Sudden Elegancies

Growing up in Hull
Living in Scotland

Tricia Levack

Design and Production by Black Tree Publishing, Hull
Gemini House, Lee Smith Street Hull HU9 1SD
Telephone: 01482 328677

Printed by: Fisk Printers, Hull

Loveark

lovearkcreative@gmail.com

Dedicated to my beloved husband
and Anam Cara,
Allan

Contents

Foreword

'The privilege of a lifetime is to become who you truly are.'
(Carl Jung).

The reason I am writing 'Sudden Elegancies: Growing up in Hull, Living in Scotland' is because I got married in 2012 for the first time at the grand age of 52 and moved to Scotland. On a daily basis I tell stories to my husband about my life in Hull when I was growing up. I realise I have lots of stories, positive and happy, about my childhood, teenage years and adult life.

I have really enjoyed telling my stories and I think my husband has enjoyed listening to them. It's brought back many a happy memory of my life in Hull. I decided that I would write my stories down in the hope that other people may enjoy them too. It has been very therapeutic for me, giving me joy at remembering what a wonderful life I had and still have, and I love returning to Hull whenever I can. I was considered to be 'poor' by economic standards, but I now realise just how rich I actually was.

My mam met my dad, where she lived in Campbeltown on the west coast of Scotland, during the Second World War, and after they married she moved to live in Hull, (where my dad was born), in 1942.

I have called the book 'Sudden Elegancies'. This is a phrase taken from Philip Larkin, when he talks about Hull and says, 'For Hull has its own sudden elegancies.'

My own life, despite the obstacles and pain that life can bring, has been full of 'sudden elegancies,' taking me by surprise, and leaving me with beauty, peace, love and hope.

I love Hull. I love its people and its layout. I love its history and its determination.

I look at this book as a social history; where I fit in the world, in Hull and the events that have shaped Hull and me. It has taken me more than three years to write. I know I have missed out lots of things as they fade from my mind, and there have probably been great events in Hull that I have missed, purely because I had no knowledge of them, for whatever reason. I have never seen the Lord Mayor's Parade, for example. Also, there are many wonderful songs and music out there over history too numerous to mention, but they have been so much a part of my life.

I've generally focussed on what has been good in my life. What has been 'bad' could perhaps be the subject of another book. But in this book, I wanted a 'feel-good-factor'; a joyous book about Hull, and other places that have shaped my outlook. Although, I do include times of distress in some chapters of the book, because, as you know, life does have its challenges.

In Part One, the focus is really on Hull as a city, but also as a personality; that is why I haven't used too many names in the book, for one, I don't want to embarrass anyone, and two, I don't want to distract from Hull as the main character of the book.

We all have our stories, and they say there is a book in all of us. I hope you enjoy reading this and I'm sure, if you are from Hull, you will see similarities to your own life.

Chapter One is My Dad's War that I have included near the beginning of the book, because, if my dad hadn't survived the war, I would not have been growing up in Hull in the first place. I also believe that it is important to remember what our ancestors went through and they may give clues as to why we are as we are. I included some of this chapter in a self-published book called, My Kintyre Ancestors…and memories of Campbeltown, 1921-1945, (written under my maiden name, 1997).

'During the Second World War Hull suffered great damage and loss of life. Hull was the most severely damaged British city apart from London. 95% of houses were damaged and 1,200 people killed between June 1940 – 1945.' (https://en.wikipedia.org/wiki/Hull_Blitz).

When my husband and I return to Hull to visit, we always go to our favourite parts of the city. I can point to buildings and areas in Hull, shops and houses and tell a story, usually funny and happy stories. We do the rounds of Hull whilst we're here. All my favourite places have become his favourite places. The town centre for shopping and galleries, the art gallery, Maritime Museum and the Museum Quarter in the Old Town; East Park, Newland Avenue, Beverley Road, Cottingham Road, Holderness Road and all areas associated with my life and growing up in Hull between 1959-2012. We also take day trips to Hornsea, Bridlington and Scarborough, Cottingham, Beverley and York.

In Part Two, I look at living in Scotland. I met my husband at the Chisholme Institute in the borders of Scotland. We both attended the second six month course in October 2010, but I first met him there on the 4th July 2010, when I went for a week long course.

Also in Part Two, I look at how I managed to survive once I got back to Hull after retreating from the world for six months, marrying and moving to Scotland and nearly losing my life to cancer and sepsis in February 2017. In Chapter 10, I look at Hull today and what you can see if you came to visit. I've not included everything, as I don't know everything. I've just included places and things I see when I go to Hull, but the list is not exhaustive. If you want to know more about Hull there are a lot of marvellous books out there and one in particular that I found interesting is a book called 'Hull: Pevsner City Guide,' by David and Susan Neave. In the last chapter of the book, I talk about my life in Kirkcaldy, Scotland.

I married at the age of 52 in November 2012, so I had lived in Hull for 52 years at that point. Originally, I wanted to write this book and have it ready for the beginning of the 2017, when Hull became the City of Culture, and the book was going to be purely about Hull, but this has changed, because I was diagnosed with cancer in 2016 and had to put off the date of publication, as I underwent various tests and operations. The book has therefore become more than just about Hull; it has become more a book about my perceptions of life and at the beginning, how Hull has been a great part of my life.

It is a different book to my original plan, because I now feel that this is probably the only book I am going to write and I want to include my time in Scotland and what happened after I was diagnosed with cancer.

In 2017, Hull became the City of Culture. Well done Hull! You have nurtured me through the years, you have seen the best of my times, and you have seen the worst of my times, but through it all you have stayed strong. Demolished and rebuilt over and over, just like me. We stand strong, you and I, and will always remain positive. We are and always have been the City of Culture.

I have a lot to thank Hull and its people for. It's seen me through good and bad times, it's watched me grow, fail, succeed, fall and get back up again. Just like Hull, I've seen darker days, yet always fought back, becoming brighter and stronger than ever. We've learned together, we've grown together.

Hull is the City of Culture 2017. It is well deserved. Hull is an amazing City and has a lot to offer. I wanted to be in Hull at the start of 2017 for the beginning of the amazing year, but due to illness, that was not to be. However, I kept in touch with Hull and the activities through the various websites and news about it. It was a great year, and I don't need to go to Hull to appreciate it, because Hull remains always in my heart.

Tricia Levack
December 2018

Part One:
Growing Up in Hull

'It is the true duty of every man to promote the happiness of his fellow creatures to the utmost of his power.'
(William Wilberforce).

Robinson Crusoe Queen's Gardens, Hull

I

My Dad's War

'There is a force in the universe – call it God or Spirituality or whatever you like – that wants the victory of truth and justice. This force will help you if you are steady, humble, brave, and patient. Never, ever give up, however bad things are.' (Nelson Mandela).

23rd August, 1940
Alice Maud Garvey and her daughter Alice were stunned by the message over the wireless. Lord Haw Haw's gleeful voice saying:-
'I have sunk the Severn Leigh with all hands on deck.'
The two Alices looked at each other in disbelief.
'Our Bill's on that ship!' they gasped.
For fourteen days they didn't hear a thing, all was silent and they feared the worst. On the fifteenth day there was a knock on the door. It was the local chaplain.
'Your son has been found alive in an open boat which drifted into the Isle of Harris.'
When I was a little girl my dad used to tell me the story of the time he was in the war. He was torpedoed and ended up in an open boat for fourteen days. He was one of ten survivors of a crew of 42 men. Being young I didn't take much in about Dad's adventures. All I can really remember is that they had been starving and dad said they had been sucking fishes' eyes to get moisture. How true this was I do not know, but the vision to my child's mind was ghastly, and I really didn't want to think about it. My dad told me the story a few times, but then suddenly stopped talking about it. I do

remember that the local newspaper asked people to send in their war time experiences to be published. Enthusiastically my dad wrote about his experiences, only to be told that they couldn't use it because there were hundreds of stories like this one. I'll never forget the look on his face when he received that rejection letter. It was as if his war didn't mean anything; it was written off as just another one of those war time experiences. But I do know that my dad never fully recovered from fourteen days in an open boat and the sights he saw and what he had to endure at such a young age. It would turn the strongest man's head, let alone a nineteen year old merchant seaman.

I don't know what it was, but something kept nagging at the back of my mind to ask about my dad's ship and what exactly had happened. Unfortunately, I lost all this information when my dad died at fifty nine of cancer in 1980, when I was twenty years old, and I regretted not listening more carefully to what he had been saying.

Aunt Alice was very helpful. She sent a lovely letter detailing all the family and sent photographs of my grandmother and great grandmother. There was a separate letter entitled Bill. 'The ship your dad was on was called the Severn Leigh. I will never forget it, it came through on the wireless with Lord Haw Haw saying, 'I have sunk the Severn Leigh with all hands on deck,' but we never believed all he said, but for fourteen days we never heard anything. We were all very upset and beginning to fear the worst when a chaplain came to our house and said they had drifted into the Isle of Harris, and your dad was one of seven survivors. He had a terrible time in an open boat for 14 days and was in hospital on the Isle of Harris for weeks. He had sea boils all over his body and he was in a terrible state. All they lived on was condensed milk and sea biscuits.

He always looked very smart in his navy suit. It was a terrible ordeal for him I don't think he ever got over it, but thank God he married your mam and had a lovely family, so he was well rewarded. I can't remember anymore except that he was very brave.'

The letter whetted my appetite to know more. Would people on the Isle of Harris remember the incident? It must have been quite something to see an open boat drift onto their shores. What exactly happened? I was itching to find out.

A few days later I wrote a letter. I didn't really know where I was sending it to. On the envelope I wrote, to the library, information centre/newspaper, Isle of Harris, Scotland.

The letter I received back from the Isle of Harris was beyond my expectations. I was absolutely amazed. I received a copy of an eyewitness account of what happened and the name and address of someone who had actually seen the lifeboat drifting to shore and he was eleven years old at the time, wee Finlay MacAskill.

There was also an account by John Morrison of Northton who is now deceased. He tells the story of shipwreck survivors who came ashore at Northton.

'A ship was torpedoed 40 miles off St. Kilda in the Atlantic. The boat was torpedoed and she was sinking so they lowered the lifeboats. They lowered three lifeboats and she was sinking fast so the crew crowded into the lifeboats. The submarine submerged and then surfaced quite close to the lifeboats and the gunmen started riddling the lifeboats with machine gun bullets. Two of the lifeboats sank and a number of the crew were killed as well. Those that were still alive crowded into one lifeboat.

They had not had time to get as much rations as they would have liked into the lifeboats. There were plenty hard biscuits but there was not much water. The captain was rationing the water for each man and some of the poor souls with thirst and after eating the hard biscuits began to drink salt water. That was fatal as they went 'off their heads' and the poor captain had to shoot some of them. It was hard for the poor man to shoot some of his own crew.

After 14 days they came ashore behind the doctor's house in Northton. They only had a few day's rations of water left. They had a sail on the boat and at night they had been spreading the sail over the boat so that as the dew fell at night it was collected in water containers. When they came to the beach the sail was up but there was no one in the lifeboat who could stand up and take the sail down. They were in a poor way.

Malcolm MacAskill and Willie MacKay saw the boat coming to the sands. The news went through the village in a flash and every able bodied man that was there went down to the sands and they took the crew out. They took them to John MacKay's house – Seonnaidh Dubh as they called him – Finlay MacAskill's and the Martins. There were 14 survivors in all. They were given warm clothes and they wrapped them in blankets round the fire so they would thaw out and regain a bit of their strength.

They were all given warm drinks of hot tea. Now things were rationed at the time but there was no scarcity of food here, nor of whisky! Colonel Thomson Rye, who stayed at the Terrace in Leverburgh, came with two bottles of whisky. MacCallum, of Rodel Hotel, sent another bottle. The doctor at the time was Dr MacIntosh – he liked a drop of whisky himself.

There was one coloured man in the crew and he was very poorly. His religion was that as he believed he was going to die, he must not eat or drink. So Doctor MacIntosh made a good 'toddy' for him, opened his mouth and poured it right down. The man survived very well too!

A crowd were gathered. There was a dentist in Leverburgh at the time attending the school, and he was there. I was there and Katie Ann was there too. She was a nurse and she was able to give some help.

A naval ambulance and a doctor came from Stornoway. I would say that the naval doctor was what I would term in Gaelic 'nyaff de dhuine'! (An idiot of a man). He was ordering the poor souls about as if they were men that had been training for a fight. Now the dentist swept the floor with him! Anyway, the ambulance took those that were ill and I took the rest in my bus. Doctor MacIntosh went as well. I believe that one died in the ambulance on the way to Stornoway, but the rest survived.

The Captain, who had stayed at the MacKay's house, wrote to Mary MacKay after that but then the strain and stress that he had suffered with having to 'do away with' some of his crew took effect. He ended up in a mental home. The lifeboat was given to the township and it was sold to John MacCallum, proprietor of Rodel Hotel. The proceeds went to the township. It was later sold to someone in North Harris.'

Another eyewitness that day was Finlay MacAskill, then eleven years old and just returning from school for lunch. He writes:-

'Yes, this incident was quite something in this small village as the ravages of war was made manifest on our very doorstep. Tragedy that so many lives were lost and joy that a few managed to survive the hazards they had to overcome.

I was 11 years old at this time and was at home from school for lunch 1-2pm. I cannot give an exact date apart from mid-September. My father raised the alarm that a strange boat was heading for the beach, under sail. The 'grapevine' soon had all the near neighbours converging at the sands.

There appeared to be no sign of life on board and no attempt was made to lower the sail as the boat approached. It was a beautiful sunny day with a light breeze blowing so the boat grounded on the sands in a few inches of water.

I recall being a bit apprehensive about going too near, initially, as one did not know what to expect, but when the older people went on board and called for all possible aid, as every one was alive, I became bold and ventured closer.

The scene there was unforgettable – living dead is the only description. The captain had been lashed to the thwarts in a delirious state, owing to drinking sea water, and to prevent him consuming any more. Everyone was in a state of dehydration to almost a point of no return.

All were helped, some carried, to the nearest houses and by this time the local doctor had arrived and began treatment as was available. They all wanted to wallow in water, but this was not advisable and only sips were given much to the chagrin of the lads, understandably.

We had three of them at our house and I remember my mother remarking on a young lad of such tender age, maybe eighteen, being subjected to such an ordeal. This was probably your dad as the rest were of an older class. An older one of this three was in a bad state of delirium and did not recover despite all efforts to bring him round – he died the same evening on the way to hospital.

There were two lascars in the company, of whom one came

ashore clutching his Koran – his only possession. They only had a smattering of English and communication with them was not easy.

However, it was decided by the doctor to transfer them all to hospital, much against the wishes of the locals who were prepared to let them stay and recover more fully before sending them on a 60 mile tortuous road to Stornoway hospital.

Two small coaches were converted as make-shift ambulances and the transfer was carried out late the same evening. I don't think anyone in the village slept that night.

My mother went to the hospital to visit them and found an unbelievable transformation in everyone after a week. A week later they were all allowed home.

The reason they were so dehydrated, it emerged, was that the lifeboat had been shelled at by the submarine as they tried to get away from the sinking ship, bursting two of the fresh water tanks. It was also mentioned that they spent 21 days adrift which seems feasible in view of the condition they were in. Scraps of corned beef and hard biscuits were the only traces of provisions in the boat – hardly an antidote for thirst! It was reckoned that one more night in their condition would have been fatal for all, but favourably the weather was mild. It was also a stroke of luck that they did not run aground on one of the uninhabited islands on their run into Harris as they were at the mercy of the wind and tides.

An interesting article appeared in the press some time after this incident – a raft from the Severn Leigh landed at Halifax, Nova Scotia with only one survivor on it. Incredible isn't it?'

I went to visit Finlay Macaskill in 2007 in Inverness. I met his wife Mary as well. They are a lovely couple and we had a pleasant afternoon reminiscing about the war and what Finlay had seen when he was a young lad of eleven years old. They fed me with sandwiches, cake and tea.

To think Finlay had seen the open boat drift into the sands, not far from his house, as he was walking home from school. He also told me that the men had been shot at as they were trying to get into the lifeboats and many had been killed.

Finlay also told me of the man who swam with the Koran in his mouth whilst the bullets were shot at him. He did not let the Koran go and survived.

I remember my dad told me the story of how they thought two people were hiding food because they had something wrapped up and would not let it go. They fought the men thinking they had food and found out that it was the Koran they were holding.

An author rang me some years later of me writing about my Dad's War and said he was writing a book. He wanted details about my dad, and I told him about what I had learned. He wrote the details in a book called 'Waves of Hate'. There is more information in there about the U-boat Captain, Victor Oehrn. He had ordered his men to shoot at the lifeboats, but then suddenly 'had a fit of conscience' and told them to stop.

Viktor Oehrn died aged 90, alone and an alcoholic. Everyone suffers in war, one way or another. In the book 'Waves of Hate, p223' it says of Oehrn, 'the sinker of the Sheaf Mead and the Severn Leigh, despite having been mentioned by name at the trial of Karl Donitz, does not appear ever to have been indicted for his own alleged war crimes. The British had captured him, then released him as part of a prisoner exchange. We can only assume that at the time his involvement with these crimes was not realized.'

I was also told that the Severn Leigh was a decoy ship and had deliberately moved away from the convoy under orders to lure out the U-Boat. So my dad, a young boy of 19, was in effect a sitting duck. When the author of the book went to look for information on the Severn Leigh in the Public Record Office, all trace of information had vanished.

'…there is a bound folder, ADM199/58. It covers the history of the OA convoys, (the Severn Leigh being OA200). On the first page an index of contents appears, written in a neat fountain-pen-wielding hand. It goes OA198, OA199,___,OA201. And there is no mention of the Severn Leigh or OA200 in the weekly Naval Intelligence Reports. Perhaps we will never know the truth.' (Waves of Hate, p11).

During the war Jenny Crossan was asked out daily by the sailors who came into The Royal Café, Campbeltown, where she worked.

'Most were gentlemen and would see me home after working late at the café. Many would give me gifts of chocolates or silk stockings.'

One sailor, who Jenny didn't want to go out with kept pestering her to go out with him. One day he became so persistent that another young sailor, who was becoming a regular in The Royal Café, told the man to go away and leave her alone.

The young sailor was 20 years old William Joseph Garvey from Hull, and little did Jenny know then that her rescuer was to be her future husband.

'Was it love at first sight?' I asked Mam.

'Oh no, I didn't like the look of him at first, but as time went on, I thought he was alright. We went out to the pictures a couple of times and he wrote me letters when he was away.'

Throughout life we find ourselves in places we don't expect to be. This was certainly true of war time. Bill Garvey found himself in Campbeltown after a period of recuperation from his ordeal in an open boat. He loved Campbeltown; it was busy, exciting, and it had beautiful scenery, but what impelled him more than anything was the redhead in The Royal Café, Jenny Crossan. He had fallen in love.

He sat in the café day in and day out, hoping to catch a glimpse of her, and plucking up the courage to ask her out. His opportunity came quite unexpectedly when a sailor kept pestering her, and Bill could see that she didn't like it. He went over to the counter.

'You heard the lady,' Bill said. 'She doesn't want to go out with you. Now, leave her alone.'

'Mind your own business,' the sailor replied and continued to talk to Jenny.

Bill looked the sailor straight in the eye. 'Get out, she doesn't want anything to do with you.'

The sailor left and Bill asked to walk Jenny home from work each night in case the sailor pestered her again. One night as Bill was walking Jenny home someone hit him on the back of the head and pushed him into an alleyway and started kicking him. Bill fought back and the man ran off.

'Coward!' Bill shouted, as he saw the sailor who had been pestering Jenny run off into the night.

After months of seeing Jenny home and going to the pictures, Bill realised that this was the woman he wanted to spend the rest of his life with. One night as they walked slowly along the moonlit loch, Bill asked Jenny, 'Will you marry me?'

'I'll think about it,' Jenny replied.

It wasn't until two months' later when Bill asked her again, 'Will you marry me?' that Jenny replied, 'Yes.'

William Joseph Garvey married Janet Crossan on the 10th June 1942 at St. Kieran's Roman Catholic Church, Campbeltown, one year after he had asked her to marry him.

Jenny bought the dress in Campbeltown with clothes coupons and the bouquet of white carnations were bought in Glasgow.

In 1980 my dad died of cancer in the January.

I had been to work that day and dad was supposed to have had a routine operation, but he died on the operating table. When they operated they found that he had cancer all over his body.

When we had visited him in the hospital the previous evening, he looked marvellous, so happy. We think that was the drugs they were giving him.

He told us the story of a man who had been in the opposite bed. 'The man in that bed died at 4 o'clock yesterday', he said. He told us that the man had said, 'They are coming for me. They are coming for me at four o'clock.' The next day he died at four o'clock, Dad told us.

The last time I saw my dad, he waved to me through the glass partition. I said later, I knew I wouldn't see him again. Every time someone said 'Your dad will be alright, it's a routine operation', it looked as if black daggers were falling from their mouths – strange, isn't it?

We had moved house by this time to a 'modern council estate' North Bransholme. It was a much larger house.

One of my brothers had been attending a local Church of England church. A couple of days after my dad died, the vicar from this church came to offer his condolences. Mam and I had been cleaning the house for visitors calling and the impending funeral.

The vicar came into the living room and his head nearly

23

touched the ceiling. I stood with my mam, the vicar and a vacuum cleaner in the middle of the small circle.

The vicar started to pray with closed eyes – my mother's face was a picture. I looked at her and she looked at me. She wasn't sure when the vicar had stopped, as he seemed to stop and think and then start praying again. 'Amen', my mam said at one of the pauses, only to hear the vicar continue. She looked at me, so embarrassed, and I started to giggle. It was awful. I managed to contain myself until the vicar left.

Mam and I started laughing when the vicar had gone. We knew it was very kind of him to come and see us, but the situation seemed so bizarre. Mam was upset, 'Here we are laughing, and your dad just gone,' Mam said. That set me off laughing again – grief is a strange thing.

It wasn't until a year after dad had gone that the pair of us cried one night, wondering about life and death and where Dad was. It was only then that I realised how much Mam missed Dad. She continued to iron his shirts for a good while after he died and I continued to think I saw him in the town, or that I would go and see if he was in the betting shop, suddenly realising that he wouldn't be there. After the initial shock of death, it seems there is a state that comes over you, that makes you think the person is still there and that everything is fine.

When my dad died in 1980, two weeks after his death I was laid asleep and thought I had woken up as I could see the outline of the things in my room. I felt very hot and remember thinking, how strange, as it was the middle of February and cold outside. Suddenly, there was a rush of noise travelling from my left ear and going through to my right ear and out the other side. It was as if there was a tunnel of light travelling right through my ears, (to open them up). I heard some voices say, 'it's alright, you can talk to her now.' I seemed to be paralysed with fright, as I heard my dad say, 'hello, Treesh, it's me, it's your dad.' I really wanted to speak, but I couldn't open my mouth. My dad always called me Treesha, instead of Tricia, I think it's a Hull thing, but I'm not sure. I heard the voices again say, 'No, don't speak, she's frightened,' and then the voices were gone, the light from my ears rushing from my right ear and out through my left, as if the passageway had closed.

I cried out, 'no, no, don't go, Dad?' It was too late, it was all over. When I told this story to people, they said things like, 'what a strange dream,' or 'that sort of dream is understandable after a death.' Everyone I spoke to thought it was a dream. I'm not too sure now, but it was comforting to know that he was still around, and my dad really was the type of person, that if he could get through from the other side, he would.

I wasn't especially close to my dad. He could become argumentative sometimes and he seemed to have moods and depression. This was put down to the fact that he had been torpedoed during the war. After he died I decided to find out about that and it was quite an ordeal he went through. Had he not been found when he was in that open boat, it would only have been a few days more and he would have died, at the tender age of 19.

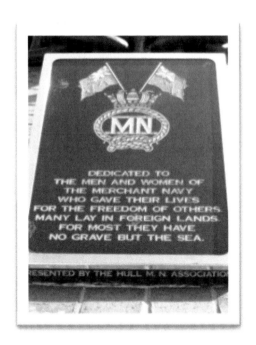

Merchant Navy, Memorial, Hull (Minerva Pier)

2

The Early Years

'…deep within us, there is a direct connection to the Divine. There is a part of our being that is beyond the personal self.' (Michael A. Singer).

I was born on Longhill Estate in December 1959. Longhill Estate was a fairly new estate, built during the early 1950s. I was born in the front room on the first floor, i.e. my parents' bedroom, of a terraced house. The house looked small from the outside, but it was long on the inside and it had a large garden at the back leading onto fields.

We didn't have a carpet on the stairs, for as long as I can remember, whilst I was growing up and the toilet and separate bathroom and the bedrooms were cold and damp. I shared a bedroom with my three sisters. There was a bedroom for my two brothers and my parents' bedroom.

At a very early age, I wondered the age old question, 'What am I doing here?' I always felt that there was something greater than me, yet something within, that was beyond me. It has been part of my life through all of my life, and no matter what happens, it has been a constant and stabilising force through the best and the worst of times.

All through my young life, I thought because we didn't have many material things as a family, that I was hard-done-by, poor, on the margins of society, but oh my goodness, when I look at the world today and the horrors we all face on a daily basis, I see now that my life was almost idyllic. I find it strange now to see how I perceived myself and my life at any given time. It seems now, that my life was full of constant sunshine and laughter when I was growing up. I can honestly say I have never wanted for anything. I have never been starving, I have always had plenty of water; I have been surrounded by love. In monetary terms we were poor, but in all other terms, I was rich beyond measure. My mam struggled to get food, although she always had soup on the go. She would ask my brother Peter to go to the butcher and ask for bones for the dog, which he got for free. We didn't have a dog. Peter also collected bottles and paper, in those days he could get money on them, and this would pay for fish and chips on a Friday for all the family. Mam said she always waited until Peter got home with the money, so that she could go and get fish and chips. My parents may have worried about where the next meal was coming from, but as a child, I didn't notice the problems.

What I remember when I was younger was the feeling of happiness as I came home from school. As I opened the back door, there would be the usual comforting sight of my mam in the kitchen, cooking a meal. It was a great feeling, knowing that my mam was there when I went home. It seemed so right and secure. I didn't know any different. It was only when Mam got a job when I was in my teens that I was most put out. Before she went out to work in the morning she used to cook the food beforehand and all I had to do was put it in the oven when I got home. It took a while to get used to because I was so used to her being there all the time.

I was quite a precocious child. I was very aware of everything around me at such a young age. I think we underestimate the intelligence of children and just how aware they are.

When I was knee high, one of our neighbours had come to the house for a cup of tea. She sat on the settee and I saw my mam in the kitchen putting the kettle on. I had a sore throat that day and I distinctly remember saying to myself, 'this will get her,' (meaning the neighbour). I went up to the neighbour and said, 'Me got headache in my throat.' She was astounded. 'Oh, have you heard this bairn, she said she's got headache in her throat.' My mam laughed. 'Yes, she's got a sore throat.'

'What a great speaker,' my neighbour said.

I knew I didn't have headache in my throat, but I was being humorous, I think. I knew I wanted a reaction, and I got one. Can that understanding really be in a person so young? I think it can.

Songs were always important to me and there seemed to be a song for every situation I was in. There was a song called 'Hole in My Shoe.' I remember it very well, as my shoes had holes in and Mam always put clean cardboard in if it had been raining or snowing. My feet were always cold. I loved primary school; it always seemed happy. Oh, there were a few instances that were upsetting as there always are, but generally, primary school was a world full of light and laughter.

I enjoyed being there. We seemed to play all the time, in the huge doll's house and the sandpit; and we sang nursery rhymes and we drew Christmas trees on bits of cut up wallpaper.

There were some great teachers in the school and it was a really enjoyable experience. Learning was and still is, very important to me. I learned how to play the recorder in primary school and how to write poetry. I also seemed to be able to create stories from nowhere.

One day a teacher read to us the story of Helen of Troy and the Trojan horse. Unfortunately, I was more interested in the hedgehog outside. I only heard snippets of the story. Something about a beach, light, wooden horse. At the end of the teacher's reading, she then asked us to write about what we had just heard. Oh dear! But instead of sitting there, I cobbled together a story from the snippets I had heard. I really got into it. I wrote pages and pages with a smile on my face, thinking I was doing well.

The next day the teacher shouted my name. I knew what this was about, as I walked to the teacher's desk. 'You didn't hear a word I said yesterday, did you?'

'I did,' I replied. And that was the truth, I had heard a word, (or two). I got a good telling off for not listening. If I had been that teacher I would have awarded the child with a star for having the gumption to write something and not just sit there and not write anything.

In another lesson a teacher asked each child to come to the front of the class and put their hand in a bag and touch an object, and without looking say what you thought it was. This was a very interesting lesson. I put my hand in the bag and thought at first that I was touching a LP record, but on further touching, I realised that it was a mirror. To this day, I have no problem finding things in the dark.

A male teacher, was teaching the class about poetry. I was seven or eight years old. He put posters on the wall of different scenes. The one I looked at seemed to be people in a medieval castle, just talking away, enjoying the moment with family and friends around a large, open fire.

The teacher told us: 'In poetry, you don't have to use words as you would do in ordinary, daily speech, you can swop them around so that the words become magical.'

With this knowledge I looked at the poster – what was happening in that scene? There was light shining in and it was a happy scene.

I noticed various things in the poster. I saw an old brown treasure trunk in the foreground. In my childish way I was going to start the poem, The sun is shining through the window and there is a large treasure trunk, but then the adult in me took over and said, you don't have to say it like that, you can use other words – so I began.

'Sunbeams gather through an open window and shine on a dirty brown treasure trunk.'

Although I can remember the poster, the first sentence of my poem is all I can remember of the poem.

The teachers thought it was a wonderful poem, and it was even published in a church magazine – it was a different church from the one I went to, so I didn't get to see it and no one thought to get me a copy. I only knew because another pupil said, 'Your poem was in the church magazine on Sunday.'

I write about the poem to illustrate that throughout my life there have been numerous instances when I've thought that words were 'given to me.' As when I travelled to Scotland at the age of three and saw the hills for the first time. The inner adult saw how beautiful they were, although I didn't know and couldn't spell the word beautiful – I saw Beauty.

I loved my primary school. They seemed to be magical years of learning. Learning and education were always important to me and I had the self motivation to take me through. I wanted to learn. I always assumed it was something that is inherent in all human beings. It was in my adult life that I realised that not everyone wanted to learn.

Our classrooms were bright and sunny and I feel that we had very good teachers. The highlights for me were the Christmas concerts, sports day (I won a certificate for winning the egg and spoon race), playing a musical instrument – the recorder, the cello (for a while) and of course, the triangle. And I loved singing; singing has always been part of my life. I have always belonged to a choir of some sort throughout my life. We used to listen to the radio at school on a weekly basis. It was very good. The teacher turned on the BBC radio programme for singing every week. It was called Singing Together and lasted for about twenty minutes. I remember some songs we used to sing, especially, 'Calling All Martians'

'Calling all Martians to take a stand,

Earthmen invaders approach our land.

Up and attack to send them all back.

We are all set, and our spaceships manned.'

I can't remember reading my first book, I only remember that my life was full of books and I loved reading. I read every book possible. How I didn't realise growing up that I was destined to be a librarian, I'll never know. It didn't even cross my mind, but a librarian I became and was so for some 21 years. Considering I've had over 38 jobs in my lifetime, being a librarian for 21 of those working years is a feat in itself.

I read constantly. I loved all the Enid Blyton books. I liked all the Hans Christian Anderson stories. All the classics. There wasn't a day went by when I didn't read. I always had a book in my hand. My mam and I used to go the 'big shops' library each week to borrow books but whenever I could I would buy my own books. We used to call it 'big shops' as it was further to walk to those shops and also had more shops than the 'little shops' at the end of our street. I used to love going to 'big shops'. It was like having a day out.

I could create whole worlds when I was younger. I was

always doing things – like writing letters all over the world. I had pen pals in France and South Korea. I made up names for myself like Rebel Miller, after Bowie's Rebel Rebel song and Toni Palmer, after Tony Curtis, who I absolutely adored and was a member of his fan club.

I had quite a few toys when I was younger, cars, dolls, and the usual games, such as snakes and ladders, and tiddly winks, but I could get sheets of paper and make a village with a post office, pub, church, and spend a happy, wet afternoon merrily talking with the local village community that didn't exist, only in my own mind.

I loved my ViewMaster with its small film reels that you put into the top and pressed the lever at the side. I travelled the world in my ViewMaster. Jigsaws were very popular too. I also had a Spirograph. These are some of the things I can remember. Some of these things are becoming popular again, and I got a Spirograph for Christmas recently, which I love.

I went into the centre of Hull on Saturday mornings. I never tired of a visit to Hull City Centre. In my younger days, and as I got older, I went to town with Mam. In my teenage years I went with friends. And apart from a year or so, when Little House on the Prairie was on the television on Saturday mornings, I never missed a trip to town on a Saturday. No matter what was happening in my life, the Hull City Centre always cheered me up.

When I was younger, a day in town, also meant dressing up in your best clothes. That tradition seems to have died off in modern society. Although some people do dress up still when shopping in town, as more and more people meet their family and friends in coffee shops, of which there are many now.

In my teens and up until C&A closed down for good in about 2001 or thereabouts; that was my favourite clothes shop. Whenever I got my monthly pay, I would buy all sorts at C&A. I remember in particular a beautiful woollen suit, jacket, skirt and waistcoat. It was very smart and didn't cost very much. I always looked smart thanks to C&A. It was a sad day when it closed in Hull.

Growing up, I had been told by my dad that there were certain shops we didn't go into because they were 'too posh'. I remember going into those shops by myself, to see what 'posh' people looked like. They didn't look too different to me, so I went in as often as I liked. These shops were Hammonds and Carmichaels.

It wasn't until I was about ten that I first went into a café, my oldest sister took me and I found it incredibly strange. I felt as if everyone were looking at me when I was eating.

The more I went to cafes the more I enjoyed it. People can look if they want to. I personally don't see what is so interesting about a person eating a meal, but that's up to them – enjoy.

I go to cafes and restaurants all the time now. I'm very lucky to be able to do that. One of my brothers calls me the café queen.

I was fascinated by the Apollo missions during the 1960s and 70s. Apollo 13 in particular stuck in my mind. How the whole world held its breath when the three astronauts were having problems in space. I love those times when the world comes together as one. I love it that on 11.11. at 11 o'clock there is a two minutes silence for all who died in wars. When 'everyone', i.e., those who have empathy, stand silent for 2 minutes. I find it very moving. In recent years however, it is sad to say, that some people look astonished and actually don't know what is going on, or know what is going on, but don't feel the same way, enough to stand still and pay their respects.

My primary school was quite a distance from where I lived. One particular cold and snowy day and the bus for school didn't turn up, my mother and I and the other mothers and children went back home, but it was decided that some parents would walk us to school later on.

I was friendly with an older girl at the school and when we walked to school later on that morning we went through the park. Lesley decided to stay in the park instead of going to school and I decided to stay with her.

What is more attractive to a young person, swinging on the swings and sliding down a slide, or sitting in a classroom on a cold, miserable afternoon?

The parents took the other pupils to school and about ten minutes later the head of the school Sister Mary St. Anne came rushing to us, her wimple flying annoyingly in the wind. 'How dare you.' She shouted. 'Come back to school immediately!'

I got up from the swing to obey, but Lesley didn't, she wasn't going to go back to school; the nun chased her round and round the roundabout, until eventually Lesley ran off into the distance and home.

I was secretly smiling and so admired Lesley, because I knew she would be 'in for it', but she chose to follow her feelings. It was wrong, I know, but in that moment, she was free, and I loved the feeling of freedom.

I knew my punishment was to come as I was dragged by the hand and marched back to school, feeling such a sorry wretch.

There were some inspiring teachers at school, and some

of the things they taught me stuck. The teacher who held up a bottle with liquid in it. 'Some people, if they have a negative outlook on life will say 'this bottle is half empty', they are being pessimistic. Others will say, 'this bottle is half full,' they have a positive outlook on life, and this is called being optimistic.'

I thought, I am always going to be optimistic and see the bottle half full, and I think mostly, that has been the case.

I was always the first child in the class to carry out research. I loved it.

A teacher asked us to write a letter to ourselves and post it to see how long it took for us to receive it.

I wrote a letter that night, put a stamp on it and posted it. I received it two days later. I excitedly told the teacher, showing her the post marked stamp on the envelope and feeling really pleased with myself.

Another teacher asked us to find out about Theseus and the Minotaur.

The following week I was standing outside class in a line with the other pupils and asked everyone if they had found out about the minotaur. No-one had.

'I have,' I said, smugly.

'No you haven't, no you haven't,' they started chanting.

So I told them there and then about Theseus and the Minotaur.

'Don't be stupid,' they said, 'you're lying, you're lying.'

I was very upset by this until we got into class and the teacher asked us who had found out about Theseus and the Minotaur.

I put my hand up and she asked me to explain. With a huge smile on my face, I proceeded to tell the class about it, exactly what I had said standing outside the class.

The teacher praised me for finding out the information.

I looked around the class at everyone with a 'I told you so' look.

It was at Junior School that I began to see the differences between those who had and those who had not.

I had friends at school, but was aware within myself that I stood apart from others, maybe because I was 'poor'. There were a group of what I would call the 'in-crowd;' girls who were very modern, confident and had groups around them all the time. They were always well dressed and had the modern shoes and coats that cost a lot. One girl was very popular with the girls and the boys. They went out dancing on Saturdays to special places open for children, and to the cinema, things that my mother couldn't afford at the time. I was never part of that group.

In those years I contented myself with the fact that I had a wonderful family. At the time my two older sisters were married and I travelled to Newcastle to stay with my oldest sister in the holidays. I loved it. I sometimes went to Newcastle town centre by myself. I went to the Civic Hall to see the sculpture of Neptune on the wall, spouting water from his hands. It was fascinating. Newcastle, at that time felt like a second home to me.

My other sister worked in a clothes shop in Hull, and she would bring me some lovely clothes home, so I was dressed nicely as I got older.

When it came to moving to senior school, it came as quite a shock, because I didn't realise the group of friends I had were all moving onto different schools – so I became even more isolated than usual.

Sometimes, I hated going to school, I wanted to be free, to have money, and do what I wanted to do.

One day, when I was in my last year at junior school, I decided that I didn't want to go to the maths class that day.

My sister from Newcastle was staying with us at the time. In the kitchen I changed out of my uniform and put jeans on and my nice weekend coat. I shouted bye to my mam and sister.

I decided that I was going to go to Hornsea for the day. I didn't know the time of the buses or anything, and I didn't realise that there were no bus stops on the country lanes, you just had to put your hand out to stop it, so a bus went past me as I walked along.

I decided to walk the whole way to Hornsea, approximately, 14 miles.

On the other side of the road a car went past that was driven by my uncle and my gran was sitting in the front passenger seat. We weren't close, so I didn't wave and neither did they. I was born on my gran's birthday, I didn't know that until I was much older. I thought it was strange. Had I had a grandchild born on my birthday, I would have made such a fuss about them, but I wasn't even acknowledged, apart from maybe to be poked fun at, if I ever did go and visit gran. As I continued with my walk, I saw a police car pass on the other side of the road, I was relieved when it went past.

Suddenly, a car stopped in front of me.

I did everything I was told not to do. I got in the car. A man was driving and I said I was going to Hornsea, he just said yes. He didn't speak the rest of the way, and when I got to Hornsea he just dropped me off near the sea front and went on his way. I shudder to think what could have happened, and I have my own theory as to why he gave me a lift. That is, I think he may have seen the police car going in the opposite direction as well, and thought in some way that he was helping me out. I don't know that for sure, but I was very grateful to be off those country lanes and near buildings and the sea. When I got to the sea front, I sat on a bench and looked out to sea.

It was so beautiful. There were a large group of school girls on the sand, in their uniforms, with their teacher, they were laughing and running. They looked so happy. I had pangs of jealousy, oh to be that happy at that moment, to be part of their group. The sky was so blue with white fluffy clouds. As I sat, something inside me made me look around.

The policeman that I had seen earlier going past in the car, was now walking towards me. He had his head down, so didn't see that I had noticed him coming towards me.

I turned around and looked to the heavens. 'Oh please God, help me, help me.' I pleaded.

The policeman approached. 'Hello,' he said.

'Oh hello,' I said nonchalantly, surprised, but not too distressed by it. (even though I was shaking inside).

'What are you doing here?' He asked.

'I'm having a day out in Hornsea'

'How did you get here?'

'My uncle and gran gave me a lift.' I said it oh so calmly, and fluently, that I'm sure that's what convinced the policeman.

'Oh, I see'. After asking me a few more questions, and me ducking them very well, he said, 'I'm sorry to bother you, but I've got to follow these things up, you understand. I saw you walking along the country lane and I wanted to make sure you were ok. Well, you have a nice day.'

'Thank you.' I smiled.

When he was gone, I breathed a sigh of relief. 'Thank you God. Thank you, thank you, thank you.'

I sat for a while, languishing in my freedom and thinking

about the horror had I been dragged back to school that day. All I needed was one day alone.

I have good memories of junior school; there were some bad memories as well though – like the student P.E. teacher who made me do a handstand and tumble right over. I couldn't do it. I could do the handstand, but I just couldn't see how my body could go over and roll and land safely. The teacher said that I had to do it for the following week.

My friends and I practised for the full week until it was time for me to do it. We practised on the fields in the break times. Every time I landed on my hands and put my legs in the air, my friends would take my legs and take me over. When I came to do it on my own, I could never do it.

My friends were afraid for me and I was afraid for myself when it came to PE the following week and the teacher made me do the handstand and roll in front of the class. I didn't think of telling my parents or other teachers as in those days, you just assumed the teacher was right.

The whole of the class held its breath as I stepped up to the floor mat. I could feel my legs go into the air and stay there for what seemed to be forever. I did go over, but flat out and my whole body fell heavily onto the mat. I felt the pain. I heard the gasps. I just laid there whilst the teacher went onto something else. She didn't acknowledge what I had done and she never asked if I was alright. It was never spoken of again.

All I can say is it is a good job I was ok or her career would have been in ruins. I don't think, or I'd like to think that a teacher would not get away with that sort of behaviour in this day and age. It was only years after I had left school that I thought of telling my mam about it. 'Why didn't you tell me?' she asked. 'I'd have gone to the school to complain.'

My time at senior school was not exactly successful. The first school I went to was quite far away from where I lived and my friends had gone to other schools. There were new people and it was a very difficult time for me. My parents took me out of the school to put me to another one, but the first school wouldn't let me leave that school, and so I didn't go to school for nearly 6 months. I was very fortunate that I was educated pretty well in junior school, so when I got to my second senior school, I was on top of all the work they were doing. They were in the middle of mock exams when I arrived, and I was told I could take the mock exams, but that I probably wouldn't do very well because I had just started the school. I did take them and I did better than anyone else.

In the French class I got 97% and the teacher gave another pupil 97½ because he didn't want someone from another school to do better than his pupils. I found this school quite a challenge.

There was plenty of bad behaviour, which I hadn't come across on that scale before. The classes were very disruptive, some of the teachers were not much older than us and not very bright. But the teachers I did respect were very good and were pleased with my progress. I got involved and loved my lessons. It was only in the last year, that I found it difficult to go. Pupils, especially girls, were nasty.

There were a few gangs at the school, and there was always one girl at the centre of it, that everyone else seemed afraid of. Just at the end of one lunch break a girl grabbed my necklace and said she wanted it. I pushed her away and she yelled that we were going to have a fight after school. Everyone said she was all talk and I actually never heard or saw her again. Another girl kept making snide remarks behind my back until one Friday evening, as I was happily going to catch the bus home, she was walking behind me and said something nasty. I saw red and turned around suddenly. I hadn't realised how close behind she was, and I was literally on top of her shouting at her to shut her mouth. I saw her fear. It was quite amazing. When I saw her on the Monday I thought she would be her usual, nasty self, but she never said another word to me. I was relieved and realised then that bullies are weak.

I couldn't understand how I loved to learn and yet the environment I was in was not geared to learning. It was all about surviving. One poor teacher, who was heading for retirement, just sat in front of the class with his head down, whilst the children ran riot. The teacher didn't move. I was angry, I was angry that this should be allowed. It was not fair to anyone. In 2009, I went into a secondary school to do teaching practice. I saw the same thing. I was observing a class, and the teacher was at the front with a few pupils who wanted to learn whilst the rest ran around screaming. I walked out of that class and never went back. I don't want that as a teacher. I can't believe parents want that either, yet they let their children get away with murder.

There is an argument with some teenagers and parents that 'what's the point, there are no jobs out there.' The point is, if you get as many qualifications as possible, you are in with a chance. I got my qualifications later in life, but it has stood me in good stead. I've only ever been unemployed three times in my life, all three for 7 weeks, and the years I was at college.

I can't remember too much about the last two years at school. I only knew that I didn't feel safe there. The classes were rowdy, nothing was learned – the teachers were helpless.

The English lessons were taken by what looked like a 'thug'; he was always dressed in tight jeans finishing just above the ankle; his hair was shaved close to his head and he wore 'bovver boots'. We were always quiet in his class because of how he was.

This particular day he stood at the head of the class and started to ask questions.

'Who in this class believes in God?– no-one in here I hope.' He mocked, laughing sarcastically.

Everyone sat in silence. I looked at everyone and decided to put my hand up.

'Yes, I believe in God.'

There was a gasp of horror from the other pupils.

'Oh yes,' he said. 'And what does this God look like? Is he an old man with a white beard who lives in the sky?' He laughed, and all the other pupils laughed with him.

'I'm not sure what he looks like,' I answered.

'And do you believe in life after death?' he continued in his mocking tone.

'Yes, I do.'

'And is life after death better than this.'

'I'm not sure, but I think it is.'

'Well, if your life after death is so wonderful, why don't you just jump out of the window now and kill yourself?' His face was twisted with anger. The other pupils had stopped laughing.

I looked the bully straight in the eye. 'Because it says in the Bible, 'Thou shalt not kill.' I said very calmly.

We continued to look each other in the eye until he just grunted and went onto something else. I breathed a sigh of relief that the interrogation and bullying was not going to continue.

Afterwards a girl said to me, 'You shouldn't take him on, he always wins.'

I said, 'He took me on, and he didn't win, did he?'

I wonder about that incident now and I know that a teacher would not get away with that nowadays. Well, I hope not anyway.

So the days at secondary school were not conducive to my love of learning. It was only when I was away from school that I became alive again. I left school at the Easter of 1975, when I was 15.

All the qualifications I gained were in my later years, gaining a degree in 1983 and an MSc in 1992, and all other qualifications such as English literature and Maths, I gained throughout the later years. I knew I could do it, and fortunately, school hadn't put me off learning. Every day I learn something new. I had loved school in primary and junior school, but the senior school was a nightmare. I would play truant whenever I could. I used to take the ferry to New Holland and have a glass of sherry whilst I was crossing. I was safer there than I was at school.

Christmas was always a very special and exciting time. It felt warming and happy. I always loved Christmas.

I always loved Christmas as a child, well, I still do, but as a child somehow, it was more magical. I loved the story of Jesus, The Three Kings, Mary and Joseph. We always had a nativity play at school. I was an angel one year, a fir tree another year, and sang in a choir another year. These are just the ones I remember. I loved it. Mam was usually in the audience, and I would wave to her.

As a family we all went to Midnight Mass. I loved the carols beforehand. It's probably why I still sing Christmas carols in a choir to this day.

Being at school around Christmas time was always exciting. It seemed always to be full of glitter and glue; Christmas cards and laughter. Outside was dark, but inside was full of light.

Outside my bedroom, (that I shared with my two sisters, after my oldest sister got married,) there was a cupboard on the landing; it was a cupboard, that generally I never went into. On this particular morning I looked in the cupboard, not daring to believe what I had just seen, I couldn't believe my eyes. There was a beautiful dolls house. I closed the door of the cupboard quickly. I didn't want to say anything, but I asked my mam about the dolls house. She was scared and horrified. 'You mustn't say anything about the dolls house. It's yours, Malcolm is making it for you as a Christmas present, but you shouldn't know about it, so act surprised.' Malcolm was my sister's fiancé, now husband. He is a skilled carpenter.

Of course I would keep it a secret, but oh dear, how young children let things slip. I was sitting in the kitchen about three weeks before Christmas and I was excitedly talking about Christmas and how I was looking forward to playing with my doll's house. Ooops. I gasped as I realised my mistake. I could see my mam look at me, like 'Oh no' and my sister shouted, 'What doll's house? What do you know about a doll's house?'

'Nothing.' I lied.

'Oh Ann, she saw it when she opened the cupboard door.' Mam said.

Ann was most put out. 'Well you're not getting it now anyway.'

I did get the doll's house for Christmas and it was wonderful.

I would go to the shops and get furniture for the house and little dolls. It was a great dolls house and I was very grateful for it.

On my birthday once my brother Paul took me to the market outside Holy Trinity Church, now Minster, in the Old Town. It was a snowy and dull day, but the excitement of the market was palpable; the smells and sounds were wonderful in my six year old's eyes, and I always loved going places with my brother. He bought me a doll's tea set and it was absolutely beautiful.

I love the lead up to Christmas, even today, maybe it is because I was born around that time, because I always feel at my strongest in the month of December.

3

Starting Work

'I believe that working with good people matters because then the work environment is good. If there is a sense of respect and belief among the people you work with, that is when good work is done.'
(Ranbir Kapoor).

I left school in the Easter 1975. The number of jobs I have had over my life were about 38. I have lost count. It was easy to get jobs when I was younger. I could walk out of a job on the Friday, go for an interview on the same Friday and start a new job on the following Monday. There did seem to be plenty of jobs around then. You usually got a job as well because someone liked the look of you and could make a decision in the first five minutes as to whether you would fit in or not. Completely different to nowadays, where you have to be all singing and all dancing in the interview. I can't remember the first job title, it was down near the abattoir and they made curtains I think. I was ok in the office typing letters on a big old typewriter, but I had to make tea for two women in the small room where they were making things. I happened to be late one day with their tea and they went berserk, calling me stupid. They were very nasty. I didn't like being spoken to like that so I left. I didn't tell the manager why, just that it was too far to travel, and because I knew I could get a job fairly easily, I didn't feel too concerned. It was a false start, and I wasn't going to mention in another interview that I even had that job.

I went for various posts, such as in the office in Hammonds. I went for the interview and was told to come back the next day. When I went back the next day, a girl was already being interviewed – someone who had a relative working there.

I was told I hadn't got the job as they had given it to the first person they had interviewed. I have learned throughout my life that it isn't fair – never was and never will be.

The next job I got was an office job. It was very strange. I did what I was asked to do, and they got a new printer for the address labels. We learned how to use it. The printer came down hard and flat. One evening, as I was using the printer, I was distracted and the machine squashed my hand flat, but I managed to pull it out quickly, making a mark on the plastic front. I was just thankful my hand was ok. I don't know how it was, but it was.

I never told anyone of what happened and I thanked God I was ok.

There was a secretary there called Mrs Onions, pronounced O'Nions. Everyone who rang up asked to speak with Mrs Onions. You heard her consternation saying 'It isn't onions, it's O-Nions.' I used to laugh silently to myself.

She was supposed to attend a shorthand class, but they wouldn't let her go on it in works time, much to her annoyance. I thought to myself at the time, that I could do with going on a shorthand course, so I found a private class not far from where I lived.

I had been off work sick for a few days and my first shorthand class was on the last evening I'd been sick. I was going to go to work the next day, so I didn't think there was any harm done.

Everything was going so well, with about 6 people in the class. About ten minutes into my lesson, the door bell rang and the teacher went to answer.

I heard a familiar voice 'Oh hello, 'I'm Mrs O-Nions.'
I nearly fell off my chair, in seconds I tried to think of how I would hide from her. Could I hide behind the curtain, could I leave by the back door, could I go to toilet and then make my escape? All useless thoughts, as Mrs O-Nions walked through the door smiling, and her face suddenly scowling when she saw me. 'Hello,' I smiled. She gave me such a look. When I went to work the next day, I was called into the manager's office and he gave me notice to leave – saying that I would be paid to the end of the month. I was too young to be devastated. I was actually quite relieved. I didn't know what was happening, and I didn't get a chance to explain. I have always believed Mrs O-Nions didn't like the fact I was attending the same shorthand class as her, and so she landed me in it.

The good news was I received a massive pay packet because I had 4 weeks holiday outstanding. I bought the brown leather boots I had always wanted, and I was free.

I went for another interview for the job of Office Junior for an asbestos and gasket company. I believe I got the job because I looked like the secretary's daughter. The money was great as it was a firm with the Head Office based in London, so I got £108.00 per month. Considering I could buy a whole wardrobe of clothes in C&A for £10.00, at the time, it was a lot of money in 1978.

I loved that job and it lasted for two years until I got itchy feet to do other things.

I worked for another gasket company on Hedon Road for a year or so. There was just me and the boss; a very sweet, old gentleman, but he was probably not that old, although I heard he died a few years after I worked there.

The building was very old and scary and the office was on

the first floor of a dump, is all I can describe it. I think it was an old railway station.

One day, when I was sitting down typing and the boss was out delivering gaskets, a small (very small) mouse crawled along the skirting board. I saw it and screamed standing on the chair at the same time. I rang home and as I described this small mouse to my dad; he was screaming, 'get out of there, get out of there,' because as I was describing the mouse, my dad imagined a giant rat, its eyes becoming as big as saucers and its tail as big and as long as armadillo.

I put the telephone down and watched the mouse run towards the tiny hole in the wall. It looked at me pleadingly every time I screamed. Unbeknown to me, dad had telephoned the police – I was still standing on the chair when a policeman stormed into the office asking if I was alright.

'Yes, I'm, fine.'

'Where's the rat?' He asked.

'It went through that hole,' I said.

He looked down in disbelief - 'that hole?', he said. It was the tiniest hole. 'I don't think it will hurt you,' he said and left.

I was still standing on the chair and as I looked out of the window, the people sitting on the top deck of the bus were all staring back at me bemused.

I've tried to count how many jobs I've had in my life so far. I reached about 38, and I know there are more, but can't think of them. These include summer jobs and temporary jobs. Considering I worked at the University of Hull, Brynmor Jones Library (of Philip Larkin fame), for 17 years, that is a lot of jobs in anyone's book. (Pardon the pun). When you think that there are many young people today leaving school who won't work until they are in their 20's and 30's, and they are expected to contribute to their pension plan and save for a deposit on a house, or pay their university fees and living expenses.

It was so easy to get a job when I was younger. You didn't have to go through the frustrating process that you go through now; writing cvs – filling in endless application forms and quite often never getting a reply from the company. If you do happen to get an interview, they don't get in touch to say you haven't got the job.

Considering we have email nowadays and how easy it is to send a message, there is no excuse for a company not to reply to the unsuccessful applicant.

There is an argument that there are too many applicants to reply to. This is no excuse. I wouldn't want to work for a firm who don't treat people with respect. What does it take?

From leaving school at 15 and taking out the time I have been at college and University, I have only been unemployed three times for 7 weeks and two of those whilst living in Scotland. There are very few jobs in Scotland, I have found. I would like to work in Kirkcaldy where I live, but this is proving very difficult. Edinburgh seems to be the place with the most jobs, but travelling would be a problem. If I had to though I would travel to Edinburgh.

What has been of most use to me when applying for a job is the fact that I can touch type. This has been a great asset to me all my life. So I would say to anyone, get typing under your belt; know your way around all Microsoft applications, Word, Excel, PowerPoint etc, and you should be able to pick up some sort of job.

Work has been a major part of my life, and for the most part I have enjoyed the jobs I have done. The only reason I didn't like them was usually something to do with other people. The jobs could be made miserable if other people treated you badly. For the most part I could stick up for myself, but sometimes I just couldn't be bothered, and generally moved on. As Jesus said in the bible, if you are not welcome in a place, shake the dust off your feet and move on.

I always seemed to be the youngest person in the job and then, suddenly, I seemed to be so much older. It was very strange, especially when the country was going through the economic crisis in 2008. Jobs were very scarce and many of the younger people would taunt the older people; i.e., those over 45 years old, and say that they shouldn't be working as they should let the young people have their jobs.

It was all quite sad. I had to work to pay my mortgage and other bills and I was living on my own, to be constantly told I shouldn't be working was heart breaking, especially as the Government has raised the retirement age. It is sad to think that many older people will be bullied out of their jobs.

I am in agreement about the young being employed. It makes more sense that the young of society should be employed. I know some young people who left school and have never been in employment, only getting work over the age of thirty. By that age I had been working for 15 years.

I know people are living longer, but even in retirement people are paying tax, it makes more sense to give young people a chance at work.

I retired myself, due to ill health in 2018, I have worked for over 38 years, but I can't get a state pension until I'm 66, and I may not even reach that age. I talk about this more in Chapter 13.

Because I came from a working class background, I was always very unsure of myself. I was extremely quiet around strangers, and it took me ages to get to know people and feel comfortable with them. I never aspired to anything greater than a typist, because I felt that I wouldn't be able to do other jobs, such as be a supervisor or lead a team. I desperately wanted to do it, but I also liked a quiet life. I liked to be able to do my job and then go home in the evening and forget about it. It worked for me.

I loved studying, so I always went on to do higher degrees. The first opportunity I had to get a higher paid job was when I worked at the University of Hull, in the Brynmor Jones Library. I had been working there a number of years as a Senior Library Assistant, a job I thoroughly enjoyed. There was an opening for an Information Skills Trainer. There didn't seem to be anyone else going for the position, so I took the plunge and applied for it. I had to give a presentation and then go for an interview. The presentation went really well, and even though the interview was slightly dodgy, I did get the job.

I was thrown in at the deep end, teaching information skills to mainly nursing and midwifery students and gradually all students and staff at the university. I had lots of self doubts to begin with, but I stayed in the job for four years, until I became ill. I still keep a payslip to this day, to remind myself of how much I earned a month, because I have never reached those dizzy heights again, for many reasons. I'm so chuffed, that for a while, I had reached high in my profession and I loved it.

I lived quite a way from the University, so I bought a flat ten minutes walk away. It was marvellous. It made such a difference. It meant that I had more time to myself instead of travelling all the time. It was lovely owning my own flat and worked out very cheap to run which was great, as I could go on my course in Scotland and still manage. I talk more about my courses in Scotland in Part 2.

I loved my working life. I did many different things and worked with so many amazing people, even the horrible ones. I don't make excuses for them, but we all have our problems and no one more so than a bully. Everyone hurts in one way or another.

We spend a lot of our time at work. For many of us, we work for very little pay. Today, some families have to rely on food banks, even though they are working. It is sad that in a society such as this, which has a lot of money, it allows people to struggle in this way. In all my years on this earth, I have never seen so much poverty, so many homeless, so many people struggling to pay bills. What has gone wrong and who can fix it? In my younger years of life, there was always hope, but there seems to be no hope in certain areas of society today, because people are not listened to. I can only pray that the Government and communities will begin to work together to help and support each other. There is money out there; there is the will to help and to improve our society; we need to work together.

Time is short!

4
College Years

'Education is the passport to the future, for tomorrow belongs to those who prepare for it today.' (Malcolm X).

It was a beautiful summer day, I was in town with Mam and I had come to a decision I was going to take a degree course at the Hull College of Higher Education.

I had struggled during my teens. I didn't have any qualifications. I had left school at Easter time to work, as I found school particularly difficult. But I knew if I got the right course for me, I would love it.

I asked around and was eventually pointed in the direction of Hull College of Higher Education on Inglemire Lane. I was fortunate enough to get on the BA (Hons) Combined Studies course in History and Religion; two subjects very close to my heart. I turned twenty one in the December of 1980, so I could start the course in the September of that year as a mature student. Had I been twenty one on the 1st January 1981, I would have had to wait another year.

By the time I started the course in September 1980, I had worked continually for five years in five positions.

I needed a reference to get on the course, and I rang my old headmaster.

He wasn't very complimentary. 'Well, you didn't do very well here as far as I remember. I'm not sure you could cope with more study.'

I pleaded my case.

'I have worked for five years and I have matured. I'm not the person I was at school. I am very capable of study and study that I am interested in.'

It must have worked because I got in college.

When I started college, Hull College of Higher Education, Inglemire Lane, (now razed to the ground), I was in seventh heaven.

The grounds were absolutely beautiful. It had once been the teacher training convent owned by the Sisters of Mercy. I was on a full-time course, yet I was amazed at what little time we were actually in college. Most of the time was given to writing essays and researching.

If I wasn't in a seminar or lecture, you could find me in the library. In the library there was a mezzanine floor with individual study booths looking out onto the grounds full of flowers and trees. I loved them. It was so peaceful. I could sit there for hours studying, reading and writing and dreaming of freedom and of all the things I wanted to do. I had a grant, (which bought me my first bedroom carpet), I was being paid for something I loved doing. It was sheer joy. It was a three year BA (Hons) Course in History and Religion, but the first year I also took English, which I dropped in Year 2. The students took three subjects in the first year to see what we would prefer to concentrate on in the second and third year. I had a feeling that my 'purpose in life' was to be a religious studies teacher, so I opted for religion in Year 2 with the core subject of socio-history.

I did enjoy the English though, as I learned so much about poetry and the great classics. I read Mary Shelley's Frankenstein for the first time, and thought it was absolutely sublime writing. I was introduced to the poetry of Gerard Manley Hopkins, T S Eliot, William Blake, Percy Shelley, John Keats, John Milton and William Wordsworth, to name a few – it opened up a new world to me and I was in heaven.

During the first year I enjoyed it so much, I hardly did any work – it was one round of going out for the evening to the student union bar and visiting people and going to see my family. In particular I went to visit one of my sisters and took my nephew out places – he was six when I was studying at university. We had great fun.

At my graduation in Leeds, 1992

The freedom at college was amazing, until it came to the first exams in June, with three weeks to go I realised I hadn't done enough studying. So, with head down, I studied more than I had ever studied in my life, and I did very well.

The old-worldly college, was connected with the convent next door. There were many ghostly stories about the college that I heard throughout the years by many different people, all of whom I knew to be very down-to-earth people.

A woman who worked in the library had been working there one evening and she heard a lot of talking and laughing in between the stacks of books of the mezzanine area of the library; she went to tell them off and stuck her head around the bookcase and said 'Will you be quiet!' To her amazement, there was no one there and the talking stopped instantly. She was very shaken by this.

Other people had seen nuns from the knee upwards, and the floor in that particular area of the college, had been raised from when the nuns stayed there. I didn't see anything myself, which I was pleased about, as I don't like anything spooky.

During my time at college, I also decided to take my 'O' levels and gained my English plus my RSA Typing Stage II exam. I had already gained my Pitman's Typing qualification at school; the only exam I took at school. I gained my Maths GCSE at a later date, when I needed to have it to get into teacher training.

In my third year at college, I had to write a dissertation on the combined disciplines. I chose to write about the religious belief and practice on a large modern council estate, writing also about the history of the estate and compiling a questionnaire about people's beliefs. I interviewed people on the estate and also the ministers of religion in the various churches on Bransholme.

During the process, a piece was written in the Hull Daily Mail with the headline:

'Bransholme says there is a God.' It was quite embarrassing really, as we hadn't come to a conclusion about the answers to the questionnaire when they put this in the paper.

The course on religion was quite difficult at first, because I had been brought up as a Roman Catholic, and suddenly, I was learning about all World Religions. There was a real gestalt switch in my mind from what I believed and what I was learning. It was really fascinating. It was on this course, that I realised that you can have interfaith working well together, without having to compromise your beliefs (this goes for anyone of a particular faith), it's accepting the similarities and the differences of beliefs and showing respect for other's views. It can be difficult when you believe that you are right and that everyone else is wrong, or when you are told that you are right and everyone else is wrong. This always reminds me of a piece by Ibn Arabi :-

'O Marvel! a garden amidst the flames.

My heart has become capable of every form:

it is a pasture for gazelles and a convent for Christian monks,

and a temple for idols and the pilgrim's Kaa'ba,

and the tables of the Torah and the book of the Quran.

I follow the religion of Love: whatever way Love's camels take,

that is my religion and my faith.' (Tarjuman al-Ashwaq Poem XI).

I have since made friends with people from all over the world, of many different faiths and beliefs, and the one thing that we all do is respect each other and see our humanity in each other. Interfaith is not about the domination of one religion over another, it is about acceptance of others and extending the hand of friendship.

It was at Hull College that I first heard of the Beshara School of Intensive Esoteric Education, now called The Chisholme Institute. A tutor at the college was a director at the school and invited students to attend courses or just visit the place, in the borders of Scotland.

I was invited to a local study group, studying the works of Sufism, Ibn Arabi, Rumi, all of which I studied at college, so I found it very useful.

I remember the first time I went to Chisholme, I was twenty four years old. I was a very shy person, so I was nervous about going.

It was late evening when we arrived. There were a group of about seven of us.

Immediately on entering the house I noticed the peace was palpable. It was a beautiful, calm evening and something in me moved in recognition. I was home, and yet not home. It felt familiar.

The grounds and the house were spectacular to me, after coming from the estates in Hull. There were large grounds surrounded by hills and trees. At the school there was a timetable of meditation, cooking, gardening and study. I was in awe at first, so much so, I couldn't eat the meal that was provided to us on that first evening.

After the meal we were taken to the steading which were the students' accommodation. I shared a room with some of the other students. I was scared but I opened the window in the bedroom and the air smelled sweet, with the sound of birds and sheep breaking the silence. It felt so beautiful, but it was something of the unknown to me as well.

There was no television for the students and the day was spent finding out about Self and the Reason for Being.

Sitting around the large table, in the dining room, with all the other people at the house, I was scared at first but I also found it remarkable and very comfortable. This was new to me and my eyes soaked up every detail.

I felt as if I had found people who knew exactly what I was about and the things they were talking about touched my heart, and stirred my inner emotions. I wanted to know more. And that is why, at the age of 26, I took the first six month residential course in 1986/87, of which I say more in Part Two: Living in Scotland.

Education is very important to me and I loved my three years at college; I went on to do many more years and have studied all my life and continue to study in retirement, learning new things every day. I think it is important to keep the mind active.

I was very lucky to be able to pursue education at a time when I didn't have to pay for it. There were no outstanding debts after I'd taken my courses and I worked during the holidays. It was such an exciting time for me; after not having any qualifications from school and, in a way, written off, I gained so many qualifications after school. Here are some of the qualifications I gained over the years. Quite a lot, considering I didn't leave school with any qualifications, apart from the Pitman's Typing Certificate I mentioned earlier.

Over the years I gained the following qualifications:-

BA(Hons) Combined studies in Socio-History and Religion 2:1

PG Librarianship and Information Studies

MSc in Information Studies – Dissertation entitled Managing Special Collections in the Field of Religion, in University Libraries.

Teaching in Adult Education.

PGCHE – Teaching Learning and Assessment in Higher

Education and I am also a Fellow of the Higher Education Academy.

And many other qualifications in between. I have a drawer full of certificates. This is not to brag, you understand. I only had to prove to myself that I could do this, and whatever anyone else said about me not getting anywhere – they were wrong.

I took my MSc research whilst I was working at the University. I undertook a research paper that I was really interested in, and I had such a great year going around the universities and looking at their collections. If I could do this as a job and get paid, I would love to.

I loved the exams. It was a time when all the talking and debating stopped, and you just wrote down your knowledge and thoughts. I can remember the final exams of my BA course, taken in the sports hall in a thunder storm, with a large spider at my feet. I remember the very last exam. It was a beautiful sunny afternoon and when I finished the exam, I walked to the bus stop to catch the bus, and as I was walking, I thought to myself, 'What now? What on earth do I do now? It's all over.' I looked into the future and there were dark pages going on into infinity and they were all blank.

I would say to anyone who has been told that they can't do something, prove them wrong, for your own sake, not their's.

I continue to this day to have some form of study going, whether it is reading a book, to taking courses, art, singing, music, languages. You name it, I'll study it. I'm not sure though, if I could have gone to university and done all I have done in today's climate, and I understand why people are going different routes, such as apprenticeships. Whatever works for you, the majority of young people I have worked with want a job and money, not having to pay back for a university course and be in debt.

5
Music, Theatre, Acting, and Singing

'Do you know what the music is saying? Come follow me and you will find the way.' (Rumi)

Songs and music have been an enormous part of my life. I wake up every morning with a tune in my head and throughout the day with songs past and present whirling around in my head. There have been so many wonderful songs over the years, that I would need one book in itself to list them all. I can seem to conjure up a song about any incident that is happening at any given time.

I believe the first live theatre I ever went to see was a pantomime at Hull New Theatre. I was absolutely overawed. I think I was about 5 years old, if not younger, and I'd never been to a place that was so packed with people. My dad, sister, brother and I sat on the stairs with a lot of other people, because there were no seats left. I'm certain they would not allow that nowadays, but it seemed then, the more the merrier.

I knew it was loud, there was a lot of shouting and music – it was all quite magical. And thus began my love affair with live theatre. I would go to the theatre whenever I could. Going by myself as I got older, to see Shakespeare, musicals, such as Hair, Jesus Christ Superstar, Evita. How I longed to be up there on stage, but I was far too shy around people I didn't know. I did have ambitions of becoming a singer or an actress, but I was never in the right place at the right time.

The first time that I became aware that I could sing was in primary school. A male teacher asked the class who would like to come out to the front of the class and sing a song. About five children got up one at a time and sang a song. It showed to the teacher that they weren't shy. I desperately wanted to get up and sing, but I was too shy.

When I went home that day my mam was singing Adeste Fideles (Oh, Come All Ye Faithful), and I asked her to teach it to me. I thought I could go back to the teacher and ask him if I could sing for him. I thought it would be impressive to sing in Latin.

I went back to the teacher and asked him if he would hear me sing and I went into the school hall one lunchtime and he played the piano for me. After my rendition he said I could join his choir. It was for the Christmas concert. I can't remember what we actually sang, but I remember being as proud as punch standing on the stage and singing in front of the audience. That was the beginning of my love of singing. At secondary school in my first year, I joined a small choir and we went around 'old people's homes' to sing. One of the songs I remember singing is 'Smile.'

It was when I saw Lena Zavaroni on the television that I had the inspiration. I loved Lena. She seemed really shy, yet when she sang, it was like she was the song, she came alive with her music. She was marvellous.

I entered myself for a talent competition at a Bridlington holiday complex when I was about 16. I sang 'Don't Cry for Me Argentina.'

I wore a lovely long black evening dress. My sister Linda came with me, but both of us were a bit bemused by the whole thing.

I had a backing track and before I went out onto the stage I was shown where the microphone was on stage, but as I came out from beyond the curtain, unbeknown to me, the microphone had been moved, and when I came out I was looking all over for it. I think the audience thought I was a comedy act.

Needless to say I didn't win that competition, but it did make me want to do more.

My dad was most put out that I wouldn't let him attend any of the places I went to sing. One night when I was singing at a club down Holderness Road, he popped in at the back, saw my performance and then left.

When I got home he couldn't contain himself. 'You were great!' he yelled.

I was secretly pleased that he had come to see me, because I could get an opinion, although probably biased.

After that he travelled around with me to various venues. It was very hit and miss with me when I sang. Sometimes I wanted to sing and at other times I seemed to go into myself and be far too afraid to sing.

I went with my dad once to sing in a club, that has long since been knocked down. I was so nervous, but as it happened a hypnotist was on that night and in the wings, as I was waiting to go on, he said, 'Are you ok?' 'I'm a bit nervous,' I replied. He put his thumb in the middle of my forehead, just between my eyes and at the top of my nose. 'You will be great,' he said, and then walked away.

I sang three songs. One was a Karen Carpenter's song 'Top of the World'.

I had a pretty good night singing that night after the hypnotist had put his thumb on my forehead. I was so confident and really loved being on stage. I think now, it may have been that I was so puzzled about what he had done, that I forgot my nerves. I'm not sure about hypnotism at all. I have been hypnotised one other time, and that was when I had to give a talk for the first time in a seminar on the philosophy of Jean Paul Sartre. I thought I was going to die when I was told that I was to deliver the seminar. I got in touch with a hypnotist and when he put me under, I didn't feel I was hypnotised. However, I did the seminar and I was confident in that as well. I put that down to not wanting to make a fool of myself.

I heard music on the radio throughout my younger years, but it was really my brother Paul, who influenced me, when it came to music.

He bought loads of LPs. He is eight years older than me; when I was five he was entering his teenage years, so I became acquainted with the Beatles, Leonard Cohen ….and the classics. When I first heard the Planets Suite, I thought I'd died and gone to heaven. When I first heard it I sat on the chair near the window and looked to the sky and was transported by the music. It was magnificent.

There are hundreds of songs that I can conjure up for any situation but that's what makes great song writing, I suppose, looking at the human situation and reaching out to others.

I remember when I was eight and I wasn't able to go into town by myself, but I could go to Holderness Road, which I thought was far more dangerous, because there was a huge road to cross, whereas in town I could walk around the roads and mainly stay on the path. So I took it upon myself to go into town without Mam knowing. It wasn't until I was in my teens and she said, 'I think you can go to town by yourself now.' I said, 'Mam, I've been doing that for years!' 'You bugger,' she replied.

It was on one of these occasions that I went into town that I went into a book shop and bought a children's educational book on composers. I read the bit about Handel when he was composing the Messiah. He locked himself in his room for days and his servant was concerned. When the servant knocked on the door after several days, Handel came out in a daze and said, 'I thought I saw all heaven before me, and the Great God Himself.' I was so impressed. What must that have been like, I wondered. I loved Handel there and then, even though I hadn't heard any of his music. Many years later, I sang the Hallelujah Chorus with the Scottish Opera.

At Senior school once when I had a music lesson, I stood in the queue waiting for the teacher to arrive for the lesson. When we got in the class, the lesson was about listening to the music to see what our feelings were about it.

The teacher played a piece of music on the record player and we listened. When it was finished he went around the class and asked us to say what we thought and 'saw'. I was the last one to be asked and each time his mouth dropped open in disbelief as I described 'what I saw.'

In one piece of music I saw concerned parents rushing up the stairs to comfort their child who was crying, and apparently, that is what the piece was about. There were about four pieces of music – I can't remember two of them, but on the last piece of music I said, 'I see trees, with the sun shining through and deer walking and eating grass. The music turned out to be 'Prélude à l'après-midi d'un faune,' by Claude Debussy. I had never heard the music before, but what I saw, was exactly what the music was about.

Instead of being pleased about this the teacher started shouting at me.

'You've been in here at break time haven't you and looked at these records?'

'No sir, the door was locked.'

'Oh yes,' he said.

'Well, you've heard these pieces before.'

'No sir, I haven't.'

It seems he thought I was up to no good. I wondered why he thought like that, because presumably that's what the experiment was about, and in my case, it worked.

I now see, that composers are so moved by Beauty that what they want to convey can travel in time from when they have written a piece, to the person listening, years down the line. It is what binds us – the Great Vision. True knowledge, given in music. Great writers, poets, artists, singers, all have this gift, because it flows from the one true source of life – the golden thread, winding its way through the fabric of life. Mozart, apparently, couldn't even remember writing notes down as they just flowed from him as if he were in a trance. This was implied in the film Amadeus, but there are many writers who touch on this also.

I was always in a choir of some sort or another. I was always in the school choir and then in later years joined choirs, such as the Betty Lorimer singers in Hull.

I have always loved singing, yet I knew I wasn't great, so I knew I wouldn't get very far, apart from enjoying it. I went to audition for Opportunity Knocks when Bob Monkhouse was hosting it. At the time I was working at Hull College of Higher Education and a man in the sound studio produced a tape for me with my songs on. I went to Leeds with my sister and sang, 'Do you know where you're going to, do you like the things the life is showing you?' One of the Nolan sisters was in the audience watching. I think it was Linda, but I'm not sure. It didn't go well. I sang, but didn't get anywhere. My first song choice, 'Don't It Make My Brown Eyes Blue,' did make it onto the show, sung by someone else. I should have stuck with that one. Anyway, years later I found that I was in good company – Joe Longthorne, apparently, didn't get onto Opportunity Knocks either. I had followed Joe for many years, going to his concerts in Scarborough, Hull and Bournemouth.

As far as I can remember, the first single I brought was Puppy Love by Donny Osmond in 1972. I was so totally in love with Donny, I just knew I was going to marry him. There was such mania surrounding him and I wanted to go to a concert, but obviously I didn't as it was too far away and was too expensive. I was twelve at the time, so there was no way I was going to get to see Donny and the Osmonds. I was to meet Donny Osmond many years later. I was studying to be a teacher at York College and there was a student there who got tickets to see Donny in Sheffield and no one was available to go so she asked me if I wanted to go. I had grown out of Donny many years before, but I thought it would be fun to go and see him.

When we arrived in Sheffield, we went for lunch just opposite the theatre where Donny would be performing that night. After lunch we walked around to the back of the theatre where a substantial crowd were gathering. We heard 'Donny is coming out in ten minutes.' We waited, and sure enough, Donny Osmond – THE Donny Osmond came out of the stage door with a huge smile on his face. Everyone surged forward screaming. I couldn't believe my eyes. I stood on the steps and looked at him. All my teenage feelings came flooding back into my body. 'Donny!' I screamed. Everyone stopped what they were doing and looked at me. I was standing right in front of him. I suddenly came to my senses, held out my hand and took his. 'Pleased to meet you.' I said, not knowing what else to say. He shook my hand, 'Pleased to meet you as well.' Then everyone carried on as before. I just stood there with a stupid grin on my face. What a gent.

The Eurovision Song Contest was always a big event in our household. We watched it from start to finish. Patricia Bredin a singer born in Hull in 1935, was the first UK entry to the Eurovision song contest in 1957 which took place in Frankfurt. She finished in seventh place out of ten entries with a song called 'All.'

Every May the Eurovision Song Contest became our night's entertainment. I can remember jumping up and down on the settee every time the UK got 12 points. The winning years for the UK were:

1967, Sandie Shaw, Puppet on a String

1969 Lulu Boombangabang

1976 Brotherhood of Man Save All Your Kisses for Me

1981 Bucks Fizz Making Your Mind Up

1997 Katrina and the Waves Love Shine A Light

The UK has also finished as runner-up on 15 occasions; including Pearl Carr and Teddy Johnson (1959), Matt Monro (1964), Kathy Kirby (1965), Cliff Richard (1968), Mary Hopkin (1970), The New Seekers (1972), Scott Fitzgerald (1988), Michael Ball (1992), Sonia (1993) and Imaani (1998). Since 1999, the year in which the rule was abandoned that songs must be performed in one of the official languages of the country participating, the UK has had less success, only finishing within the top ten twice. Jessica Garlick in 2002 finished joint third and Jade Ewen in 2009 finished fifth, Ewen in particular was praised after her performance of 'It's My Time' for ending the run of poor results the country had suffered for much of the decade.

And who can forget the near miss of the UK in 1988 in Dublin when Bruce Forsyth daughter's song 'Go' came second by one point to Switzerland's 18 year old singer, Celine Dion. The camera flashed to Bruce who was stunned by the

Yugoslavia's last votes. As usual Terry Wogan was being his jovial self, as we came to adore Terry on Eurovision; some people watching it, purely for Terry's wit. The song 'Go' was sung by Scot Fitzgerald and it seems appropriate today as the UK has voted to leave the EU. The UK had 136 points and Switzerland 137. At least the UK lost to Celine Dion – the world was given a great singer.

I was very shy when I was younger, yet I still wanted to go on stage. The stage musical Hair came to Hull New Theatre. I was about 18 years old. I'd gone to a performance on the Thursday evening and I saw that at the end, the cast came out into the audience and got people up on stage to 'Let the Sun Shine in'. I so wanted to go up, but was afraid. After that, I planned to go on the Saturday night and as it turned out, one of my brothers was in the audience. I'd dressed up specially, in case I managed to get on stage. It was funny, that my brother was the one they came to get up on stage, but he flatly refused. I went up in his place. One of the cast members held me by the hand as we went up onto the stage, and then everyone was dancing. I moved around and danced, but I didn't know what I was doing, I felt so self-conscious. I felt as if I was on stage for hours and just wanted to get off. As I looked out onto the audience, they sat stiffly with unsmiling faces. My first thought was, 'Oh God, I hope no-one I know has seen me.' I was really glad to get off that stage. How strange is that, to want to be seen and want not to be seen all at the same time.

I also entered a talent contest at the Hull New Theatre, and sang the winning song from the Eurovision Song Contest, of 1977, L'oiseu et l'enfant, sang by Marie Myriam, which happened to be French, so I sang in French and English. I loved it, but what I didn't realise was the theme of the talent contest, was 'all about being British'. That was said on the evening of the contest. Needless to say I didn't get in. A young boy miming to Kate Bush won third place, I think it was. He was really amusing.

To try and satisfy my need to sing and be seen, I joined a singing group called the Betty Lorimer singers. We were a lovely group of mixed gender, ages and vocals. I remember very pleasant Saturday afternoons practising our songs and then performing, once at the Library Theatre and once at a Catholic Church Hall. It was wonderful.

Thinking about it I was always in a choir of some sort. I have a love-hate relationship with singing. I know it is good for us, but I have always suffered from a cough, I think brought on because I am allergic to something I'm eating, and when I sing I always feel as if I have to clear my throat afterwards. I was in the school choir, the Betty Lorimer singers, Hull Community Choir, The Second Course Singers, Harmony Rocks, Songburds, Interfaith choir and the Rock Choir, making appearances in other choirs, such as the Scottish Opera, putting the Hallelujah Chorus together, and in Diversity week in Kirkcaldy, I joined the Interfaith choir, which was such a sweet experience.

I also played the recorder and my brother had a keyboard that I learned to play.

I performed in The Hull Community Play Vital Spark in 1992. I auditioned for Vital Spark, the biggest thing to hit Hull for years. Everyone was so excited. I wanted to be a part of something that was about my heritage and ancestry.

Vital Spark was written by Jon Oram and directed by Rupert Creed and Jon Oram. The music was by Hilary Gordon, design by Eryl Ellis and Costume Design by Chris Lee. There was a cast of around 200 people.

This was the story of Hull and its people and spanned two centuries of Hull's History.

The play included the tragedies of the 3 lost trawlers, the St Romanus, Kingston Peridot and Ross Cleveland, and the campaign headed by Lil Bilocca for better safety conditions on the trawlers.

Big Lil, as she was known, organized a 10,000 signature petition calling for reform. She led a delegation to Parliament and eventually met with the Prime Minister Harold Wilson. She and her supporters carried out direct action, trying to stop boats leaving St Andrew's Dock and even threatening to picket the PM's house if there weren't reforms. Speaking to a BBC reporter she said 'If I don't get satisfaction I'll be at that Wilson's house, private house, until I do get satisfaction in some shape or form.' The campaign was successful with many new safety measures introduced, including making it compulsory for every trawler to have a full-time radio operator.

I went to the rehearsals for Vital Spark every week, sometimes twice or three times a week, for a year. I was in the choir and I loved it. It was wonderful being a part of such an undertaking. The excitement of coming together with hundreds of people from Hull and creating a play about our City was very uplifting and I was pleased and proud to be a part of it.

I was playing a poor woman, and I was singing in the choir. It was an amazing play in many ways. It was a promenade play and the audience walked among us with four stages around the side of the theatre.

I've noticed that in my life, when I really enjoy doing something, everything seems so easy to do. I travelled across Hull on an evening for nearly a year and rehearsed on Saturdays and

Sundays; but it was all such a joy to do.

Organising over 200 people must have been a huge challenge. How they got it together is a mystery in itself and I was there; I saw it happen. I looked forward to the rehearsals at the end of a busy day at work; to go along and act and sing along with other people, all of us wanting to do well.

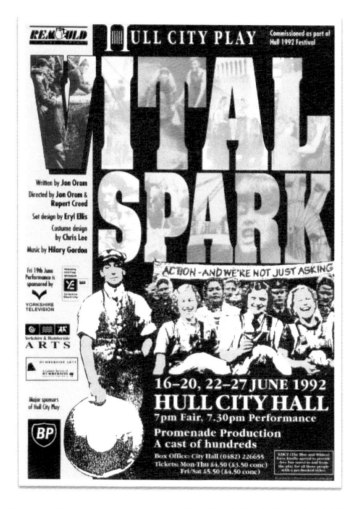

Poster for the promenade play, Vital Spark, 1992

My niece, Nikki, was in the play as well, and the funny thing is, now I look at photographs and see people I knew, but I didn't know at the time that they were in the play. Each part of the play was rehearsed separately and then eventually brought together, so I must have missed some people along the way. I know I hardly saw my niece throughout the evenings of doing the play. It was a huge undertaking, and I'm so proud to have been a part of that, if only a small part, it was none-the-less an exciting time.

It was a promenade play, so the audience was walking amongst us. That could be quite scary at times, as young teenagers elbowed me during some scenes. Unfortunately, for them, one scene was were everyone started shouting and screaming over trawlermen's rights, and I shouted at the elbow pushers, 'What the hell do you think you're doing?' I think they thought everyone was shouting at them and they soon made a quick exit.

It was the 25 year anniversary of Vital Spark on 16th June 2017.

When I moved to Scotland the first thing I did was look for a choir and I found one called Harmony Rocks, which then changed its name to The Songburds and then I joined the Rock Choir in Glenrothes which meet up during the day, so that was handy for me. It was great performing at the Edinburgh Fringe with them in 2018; very exciting.

Recently, I went to the filming of the Christmas and New Year 'Songs of Praise' at the McEwan Hall in Edinburgh. It was interesting to see how the programme was put together. It was presented by Aled Jones and Katherine Jenkins and had a few surprise guests, including Russell Watson and Susan Boyle of Britain's Got Talent fame. She was just outstanding, she was so tiny and when she sang she was captivating. She certainly has a special gift.

6

Writing and Art

'Yesterday I was clever and wanted to change the world. Today I am wise and want to change myself.' (Rumi).

I believed that I could do anything I wanted to do, such as singing, acting, and also writing and painting. I loved painting mainly in watercolour and I mostly painted religious art. I spent many a happy Sunday morning totally engrossed in painting a picture. I would sit on the floor in my bedroom paint and paper all about me and lose myself for hours. I could start at 8am and not realise how long I had sat and painted until I heard my mother shouting at about 12 noon to help her with the Sunday lunch. My degree was in religion and history and somehow it seemed appropriate to paint religious art. I even managed to sell a few.

People loved my paintings when I showed them to them. I hadn't formally learned to paint at this stage, but I still enjoy painting all sorts of things. At the moment I'm into botanical art, iconography and landscape painting. So beautiful. I cannot believe sometimes, when I look at botanical art that it is a painting and not a photograph, the detail and likeness is so striking.

My other love is writing. I so wanted to write when I was younger and I started out by writing letters to magazines, and to my surprise found that they were published. I did so for over a number of years. I'd write about anything; things that I was doing, thoughts and feelings and I enjoyed it every time I found out that I had been published.

I won a competition on a Radio Humberside programme, a

meal for two, and when the DJ was talking to me, over the telephone, he asked what I liked to do, and I told him one of the things was writing letters to magazines. I received a telephone call from the DJ in the middle of the week at work and he asked me if I would go in and talk to them about writing letters for magazines – which I did, and thoroughly enjoyed it.

A complete stranger rang me up at home and asked me if I had letters published in magazines and when I said yes, he said, 'Oh, you are real are you? I've seen your name that many times in so many different magazines, I thought you were made up.' I assured him that I was real. But I didn't blame the man for thinking that, as I had often thought that myself.

I print here a selection of the letters I wrote to magazines. I wrote all my life, such as writing daily dairies. It was about the year 1989 that I started writing letters to magazines. It is quite something to see your name in print, even if it is only a few words. I got a lot of satisfaction from it.

The first one was in 1989 for Woman's Realm, for which I received three pounds:

Fruit for thought

'I write in reply to the lady who wrote about supermarkets cracking down on people who munch grapes for sale to check them (May 30 issue).

What's wrong with checking whether the goods you're about to purchase are of a high standard?

When I went to Turkey recently, the shopkeepers always handed over fruit for me to test before I parted with my money. Even if you don't end up buying anything, they're not offended. It was like a breath of fresh air to feel wanted in a shop and be greeted with smiles.

It's about time Britain's shopkeepers were a bit more civil to their customers.'

The People's Friend, December 22nd, 1990.

'Why is it that when I was twenty-one I saw thirty as being ancient, but now that I've reached thirty I feel younger than ever and less worried about age?'

My Weekly, letter about my niece Rachael. 1990.

This was a letter about my niece Rachael, but I can't find it. It was about her sister being off ill from school and her Grandma visiting. Rachael said she wanted to see grandma as well. Her mum said you can see Grandma at the weekend, to which she replied, 'Oh no, that's my day off.'

The People's Friend, 1996

Getting Older

'I've heard it said that you can tell you're getting older because policemen look younger than you.

I found out I was older the other day when it started to rain. I took the scarf from around my neck and wore it as a headscarf and actually felt comfortable in it!'

Woman's Weekly, February, 1994

Pick of the bunch

Why not?

'People have often asked, 'Why on earth do you go on holiday with your mother?'

My mother is 72 and I am 33. Although I go on holiday with friends, I like to go on holiday with my mother at least once a year. We have great fun. We go dancing, to the theatre, to summer shows, walk along the beach and have a good laugh. My mother is extremely funny and young at heart. Why do I go on holiday with her? Simply because she's my best friend!'

For this letter I won a bouquet of seasonal flowers and a

box of Belgian chocolates worth £25.00.

Sunday Mirror, July 24, 1994 - £5.00

'Russell Grant's predictions are sometimes too close for comfort. Having just got the key to my Box 13 on my Take Your Pick card, I agonised about whether to open it. I did and got a booby prize. Minutes later I read my stars: 'You can pick a star prize or plump for the booby.'

A question to the People's friend, January 15, 1994

'Why do pawnbrokers display the three-ball sign outside their premises?

Answer: Merchants and bankers from Lombardy, Italy brought the symbol of three golden balls when they came to London centuries ago. The sign has in the past been held to be the arms of the Medici family of Florence, but this is denied by many historians.'

Catalogue and Index: Periodical of the Library Association Cataloguing and Indexing Group

Autumn 1995.

Cinderella Cataloguer

'Melvyn Barnes's 'Will the last cataloguer to leave please turn out the light?' (Catalogue & Index Number 116, Summer 1995) was very poignant.

For five years I have worked in a large academic library as a cataloguer. About 60% of my work involves cataloguing, and as far as I'm concerned I'm doing a worthwhile and challenging job, despite having to put up with the most awful professional abuse with comments such as 'A trained monkey could do your job' or 'What are you doing in a job like this, surely you can do something better for yourself?' And when you tell library staff from other institutions that you are a cataloguer the reactions range from 'Oh you poor thing' to gasps of horror and a knowing 'Oooooohhh…!!'

with eyes raised to heaven. Ever felt worthless? I really do believe that if I told people I was a lady of the night I would receive more respect.

It is an absolute disgrace that anyone anywhere should criticise another for earning an honest, decent living. I do not think that Melvyn Barnes is mistaken or being reactionary when he suspects that we no longer pride ourselves in cataloguing as an art as well as a skill and that standards have declined.

At present I am one of two full-time cataloguers in my institution. The aim is to get as many books catalogued in the shortest possible time. Hence there are numerous mistakes as time is not dedicated to quality. I am surrounded by books and really do feel like Cinderella, not doing right for anybody, being pushed one way to get as many books as possible catalogued, and then being criticised for making mistakes. What do they expect?

I have to constantly remind myself that the cataloguer is the creator of order out of chaos. The centre around which the whole of the library revolves is a well ordered, well maintained catalogue. Without it there is chaos and uncertainty. You can have guiding in the library; you can have information specialists teaching users how to find information, but if that information is not where it should be, you have nothing.

The cataloguer is the guardian and custodian to the treasury of the library, and should be seen as having a positive and creative role in libraries.'

Recently, (February 2016), I discovered that someone had used a quote from this letter for an academic book called Cataloging and Classification: Trends, Transformations, Teaching, and Training, by James R Shearer and Alan R Thomas.

I couldn't believe it. I thought I had won the lottery. Fancy someone quoting little old me in an academic book worth £47.00.

Chat, August 1997.

'When I was researching my ancestry, I discovered a branch of my family that went back centuries in the Kintyre area of Scotland. It inspired me to revisit the area after 18 years and it was wonderful to see my Aunt, Uncle and Cousin again. This research made me realise that living relatives are important and we shouldn't take them for granted. I'm grateful to my ancestors for bringing us closer.'

The Coronation Street Experience

'You don't watch Coronation Street do you?' A question I've been asked accusingly many times in my life. It makes me wonder what it is about Coronation Street that evokes so much emotion within a person.

People will deny they watch it and then proceed to tell you what is happening in the latest episode. There seems to be some sort of embarrassment about watching the programme. But love it or hate it, you certainly will get adverse reactions when you utter the words, 'Coronation Street'.

When I was fifteen I decided to take English Literature 'O' Level evening class at the Hull College of Further Education. The lecturer of the class believed that you can tell the kind of person you are and the background you come from by knowing what you watch on television. So, our first task was to introduce ourselves and let everyone know what we liked to watch on television.

'Educational programmes,' said one.

'Cooking and gardening programmes,' said another.

'And what do you watch on television?' she asked me.

I was honest. 'Coronation Street,' I replied.

I just couldn't believe what happened next. The group, comprised mostly of adults, began to boo and hiss and mutter under their breath long after I had uttered those two terrible words. I hung my head in shame. I felt as small as a pea and wanted the ground to open up and swallow me. I never did return to that evening class. I was too ashamed. As the years passed it became increasingly obvious that society states that you are a certain type of person if you watch a certain type of television programme, or read a certain type of newspaper. But can we really know what a person is like by what they watch on television or by the kind of newspaper they read? You can perhaps know a part (if that), but you cannot possibly know the whole.

I consider myself to be working class; I watch Coronation Street, but that reveals absolutely nothing of the Reality of the person I am.

I am as old as Coronation Street, and over the years I have changed and matured as it has. I no longer run away from people or situations, but more importantly, I no longer run away from myself. What people may see, or want to see on the outside, only scratches the surface of what is on the inside. It could be that people see only what they want to see.

My life may be ordinary, as the people on Coronation Street, but delve a little deeper and you will find that there is much more to me than Coronation Street.

I went to a writing class at the University of Hull, Adult Education, and had this piece written in a small booklet called: I Remember When… an anthology in search of times past.'

The Ear
'Wheat in the moonlight,
One ear alone,
Full moon shining its inner light on corn below.

Peaceful it sits, smiling,
Happy and content,
Gentle wind blowing, caressing in its flight.

It stands above all others,
Stretching its golden seed,
Cloudless sky above it,
Is all the ear sees.

Harvested, floured, made into bread,
Heat of the furnace changes the head.

Now it is Higher,
Part of the Whole,
It yields to the Other,
Though nothing at all.'

My Ancestors
'To the home of my ancestors,
A place far away.
To the land of Kintyre,
I'll travel one day.

To be with my kin folk,
To stay where they are.
Where they once roamed the earth,
Are now buried there.

Yet, alive in my heart,
They will live once again.
To their future descendants,
They will speak through the pen,
Of a writer who loves them,
A branch of the tree.
Roots of the earth.
My family.'

I wrote a few pieces for academic journals as well, 'Diagnostic self-assessment of information literacy skills for 1st year pre-registration nursing and midwifery students,' and 'Beyond the Demonstration: approaches to delivering information literacy.'

I spoke at a conference in Eastbourne for CILIP (the Chartered Institute of Library and Information Professionals), Health Libraries Group, with a paper entitled: 'Information skills assessment for 1st year pre-reg nursing and midwifery students at the University of Hull,' and I was so pleased to do it. I thought I had achieved a lot, having come from a 'poor' background, as people kept telling me. I had worked my way up and I was thankful for my love of education and learning.

I was in Eastbourne for a few days. I went the day before the conference so that I could get my bearings and there was an ice cream parlour opposite the venue where I was going to speak. I promised myself, that if I was successful at the conference, I would buy myself a huge knickerbocker glory, and I did. The next day after the conference, I sat and ate the huge mint and choc chip ice cream with wafers and looked across at the venue I had spoken at, and I felt very happy and satisfied. Quite an achievement. My hotel was not very far away as well, and every morning I went down to the sea and sat on the pebbles in the warm sunshine.

I also spoke at the annual Learning and Teaching Conference at the University of Hull, Engaging Students and I spoke on 'Approaches to Enhancing Information Skills', and was also presented here with my PGCHE certificate.

I loved researching and I would write anything and anytime I could, whether it be a diary, daily observations, poetry, or more academic pieces.

It was whilst I was writing a paper for yet another conference on spirituality, that I noticed the link between my two favourite subjects, religion and information skills. My paper was entitled 'Re:Searching – Spirituality and Religion Online.' It was whilst researching this paper that I saw the research process as being rather like a spiritual journey or quest. When you look at research and spirituality they encompass the same characteristics.

Research	Spirituality
Searching	Searching
Truth	Truth
Reality	Reality
Intimate – personal	Intimate – personal
Communal – Social	Communal – Social
Knowledge – Insights	Knowledge – Insights
Validity	Validity
Desire	Desire
All pervasive	All pervasive

I didn't get to give this talk as it was the day of my Mam's funeral.

I have also painted many paintings in my life, purely for fun and enjoyment, but I painted a few and sold them at one time for £10 each, to people who liked them. Now I am a member of the British Association of Iconographers and love painting religious art, botanical art and landscapes.

I now belong to an art group that meets every Wednesday afternoon at the St Bryce Kirk in Kirkcaldy. I just love it here as the tutor is so good and the group are the most wonderful group of people. I enjoy the banter and the laughter and the two hours goes so quickly. It is two hours of pure concentration and joy. They don't hold back on their constructive criticism, and I have a long way to go before I reach their standards. I'm blown away by their mastery.

My most recent letter was in the Scottish Daily Express, October 23 2018, and I won Star Letter of the Day and went on to win Star Letter of the Week, for which I won a bottle of Glen Moray whisky. My letter was entitled How far have we come from the struggle of Rosa Parks?

'I cried buckets on Sunday night watching Doctor Who.

It concentrated on Rosa Parks, the activist of the US civil rights movement, who refused to give up her seat on a bus for a white person.

The character Ryan was hit across the face for picking up the handkerchief of a white woman when the Tardis landed them in Alabama just before December 1, 1955.

It was heart breaking, not only because this happened then, but that it's still happening today.

I turned on my television this morning only to see a man on a flight being verbally abusive to an elderly, disabled black woman.

As a human race, we don't seem to have come very far. Do we really want a society filled with hatred? How on earth do we change hearts and minds? Watching all this, it seems as if for some people earth is the most alien planet in the universe. Let it not be.'

When I became ill and had major surgery for cancer in 2017, which I talk about in chapter 13, I suffered from post-traumatic stress disorder. I went to an expressive art class to help with the stress I was suffering. I found it a really incredible process and it was a new way of working with art. It came from within and it was very freeing. I was very impressed by how much the process helped and I felt that I had created pieces that meant so much and was created from the heart. It was the first time I had created something that I hadn't copied, bringing up all sorts of emotions to help with the healing process.

The number three kept coming up in the group. For example, I painted three owls and someone else painted three flowers. I said that the number three was the first 'real' number as it was in the number three that you could see relationships. I went away and looked it up on the internet, and what came up for me was the healing process of 'mind, body, and spirit.' It is also the Holy Trinity in the Christian tradition. There have always been twins in my family, but during this particular week of 'threes', I found out that one of my nephew's wife was having triplets.

When I was telling my husband about the number three, he looked a bit surprised. 'What's the matter?' I asked him. 'Oh, nothing.'

A few weeks later it was my birthday and we went to Edinburgh to stay for some events at the botanical gardens and my favourite restaurant, 'Angels with Bagpipes'. On the morning of my birthday, my husband gave me his presents, one of them was a book entitled, 'The Holy Trinity and the Law of Three, by Cynthia Bourgeault' Also, my niece, Sue, from Hull had sent me three wooden church mice from the Holy Trinity Church, now Minster, in Hull. I was struck by this coincidence, and the book itself is fascinating, talking about the living influence of the Holy Trinity in life; a beautiful book. The Holy Trinity is not just a theological article of faith, but expresses the very structure and method of creation at every level – how things come into being, change and evolve towards perfection. In this book it talks about Jacob Boehme who says: 'When you remain silent from the thinking and willing of self, the eternal hearing, seeing and speaking will be revealed in you. Your own hearing, willing and seeing hinder you so that you do not see and hear God.'

7

Holidays
'Once a year, go some place you've never been before.'
(Dalai Lama).

I am the traveller of the zodiac signs, Sagittarius, and my first recollection of a long journey was when I travelled to Campbeltown, Scotland, the birth place of my mother, Jenny. It was 1963 and I was 3 years old.

We journeyed through the night – sleeping on the train, upright in our seats. I was so excited about travelling. The train pulled into station and I stood on the platform. I seem to remember I was either naughty or didn't hold my dad's hand when he asked me so my dad walked away from me saying, 'That's it, I'm leaving you here, you're not coming.'

I remember seeing the back of my father walking away and in that moment I was trying to work out how I would get home by myself; by bus, taxi? And what would I do when I got there, the house would be in darkness and I couldn't get in, I didn't have a key.

It was a task beyond me, so I screamed and screamed and screamed. My dad came back to me and grabbed my hand. 'Don't be stupid, you don't think I'd leave you, do you?

There were many images flashing through my eyes as I travelled on the train – I was silenced by the magnificent mountains and just stared at them quietly.

Other images of that first long journey, were crying desperately on the first night of arriving in Campbeltown. I can even remember the feeling as I was passed from person to person to try and comfort me.

I remember my twin cousins a year or two older than me,

pushing me in a puddle, an act that their mother denied happened years later when I told her the story. 'They wouldn't do such a thing.' She grumbled.

When we went to see my grandmother, there was an air of quietness. We were told we had to be quiet. The room was dark as we entered and I can remember seeing this elderly woman sitting on the bed. As I approached she reached out her hands and grabbed me by the shoulders. She made the strangest noise as she did so – it was an approving noise at seeing her little granddaughter for the first time, and a granddaughter with the same red hair as her beloved husband, who had died in the past year. My mam also had the same colour hair.

We seemed to have a lot of school holidays. The school day ran from 9 to 4pm and I used to get home around a quarter to 5. I think this stood me in good stead when I got to work. It wasn't so hard when I had to leave work at 5.30. If I remember rightly, we had three weeks off at Easter, six weeks in the summer and three weeks at Christmas. I'm not sure about the weeks off in between, if there were any at all, but I always loved the holidays, doing exactly what I wanted to do, well, within reason and as much as my small budget of pocket money would allow.

In my mind the six weeks' summer holidays were always happy and sunny, they probably weren't, but that's memory for you.

When I was younger I used to go around with my sister (who is six and a half years older than me), much to her annoyance. It must have been awful having such a much younger sister going around with you and your friends.

We'd spend days exploring in the fields, going to the park, the shops, around to each other's houses, taking dogs for walks for pocket money, running errands for neighbours. We'd be out all day, eating wherever we could get food.

During the summer a theatre van would travel around to the parks and put on a really good show with magicians and dancers, and all the children would gather round.

I can practically remember all my summers. We weren't rich enough to travel, but as a family we might have stayed in Bridlington for a few days, where my Grandmother, on my dad's side, had a boarding house. I think I only stayed at the boarding house once, because, as far as I remember, we weren't overly welcome. I think that was because we were considered to be the 'poor' relations, but we did take day trips to Bridlington, Scarborough and Hornsea. We'd generally sit on the sand, have an ice-cream or fish and chips and go into the amusement arcades. In those days it was about amusement and not just one-armed bandits. I loved the laughing policeman and laughing sailor (there is still one at the Maritime Museum in Hull), apparently everyone stood around laughing, not at the policeman or sailor, but at me laughing at the dummy. I also loved the crying baby and the father in the night shirt trying to comfort him. There was also the night watchman where all sorts of spooky things were going on around him.

One day in the summer holidays my sister and a couple of friends went to play at the small bridge over the drain in the fields at the back of our house. I was just a bit taller in height than the small wall that went over the bridge and I kept resting my hands on the wall and kicked my feet in the air. My sister kept yelling at me to stop it or I would fall into the drain. I could see how upset she was so I kept taunting her. 'I'm going to jump in, I'm going to jump in.' My sister was upset, because she knew that if anything happened to me she would get into trouble.

Unfortunately, for me, although I had no intention of jumping into the drain, I kicked my legs too high into the air and promptly went head first over the bridge and into the drain. I can still remember the feeling of flying through the air, the sharp intake of breath at the sudden realisation that my life hung in the balance. I landed on my head on something hard, which I knew was a bicycle wheel, gargled in the dirty water and spluttered as I managed to get myself upright and sit in a daze, with weeds and sludge wrapped around every part of my body. My first sight was the frightened faces of my sister and friends standing on the side of the bank as I tried to decide if I was ok or not.

I screamed and screamed at the realisation of what had happened. Linda started crying. My family rushed out of the house, apparently hearing my screams all the way across the field. I screamed all the way home, wet through and muddy. I looked such a sight that my mam and sister Ann couldn't stop laughing, which made me scream all the more.

Linda was crying at my side. 'I didn't do it! I didn't do it.'

I kept saying, 'It wasn't her fault'.

What Linda had seen on the bridge as she turned around, was my feet disappearing over the side of the bridge.

I was put in the bath and then snuggled up in my pyjamas and thoroughly spoilt – all was well.

When I think about that now, I marvel that I came out of it unscathed, apart from a bruised ego. My sister recounts that story to her children now. Honestly, you can't get away with anything, can you?

Sunny days always make me remember my early life and teenage years. I love sunny, calm days. I find the winter sun particularly beautiful; because although it's sunny, it's cool. It feels as if the whole world is at peace and in love. In summer, the sun can make you feel very sticky.

At the end of my first year in secondary school, I took a holiday in Torquay, just three weeks before we broke up for the six weeks' summer holiday. We had to go on a two weeks' holiday when my dad's firm was shut. So I always got off school for two weeks', a week before the six weeks' holiday.

In those days it was accepted that this was the case, and the school always said yes, I could go.

I used to send my classmates a postcard.

I loved these two weeks' holidays, because I felt so free and happy.

The trip to Torquay was particularly happy as it had been a hard six months for me in my new school and my sister had just married and I was one of the bridesmaids. Somehow, we happened to be in Torquay the same time as my sister and her new husband were on their honeymoon.

I couldn't believe the beauty of Devon. It was superb. As a fourteen and a half year old I was stunned by its beauty.

We travelled all over Devon and Cornwall, going to places like Looe and Polperro and Brixham, Totnes and Paignton, to name a few.

I went with my sister and her new husband to see Sparks and I also had my photograph taken with, I believe, Pink Floyd, but I can't remember rightly.

I travelled to Devon again with my husband a few years after we got married because one of my step daughters and granddaughter lives down there. We went to see the house of Agatha Christie, Greenway. It was so wonderful to see. How I wish I could live in a house like that. What an incredible life to live.

Going back to school for the week before the six weeks holiday after being on holiday for two weeks was very difficult, although ok, as I knew I only had a week left.

I sent my classmates a postcard saying, 'Wish you were here, but glad you're not.' Everyone told me that the teacher read it out in class. He was very pleased to have received it, he told me when I returned to class.

After my dad died, I used to go on holiday with my mam a lot. We went to places like Jersey, but it was mainly local places we went to and we went to Scarborough most years and also day trips on the buses. I loved going to Haworth and Bronte country.

In Scarborough we used to go to the summer shows. I remember going to see Joe Longthorne and he held my hand and sang to me. 'To all the girls I've loved before.' I was very happy with that.

As I got older, around 10 years old, my mam used to take me to the museums in Hull. I remember one day, it was the last day of my holiday, Mam, out of the blue, decided to take me to the museums. I hadn't been to them before. The Art Gallery, William Wilberforce's House, the Transport Museum and the whaling museum. It was absolutely fascinating. I had such a wonderful day that day. I learned so much, and it was a great day to spend with my mam. I hadn't wanted to go to school, and when I started school the next day, I remembered what a wonderful day I'd had the day before and that seemed to make things so much better.

I had flown on an aeroplane when I was about 14 and then again at 18, but my first time abroad was in December 1986 when I went to Turkey on my first course at Chisholme, which I talk about more in Chapter 11. I then got the bug for travelling and went to many other places around the world; Malta, Rome, Switzerland, Ireland, (these are some of my favourite places, going back time and again). I've also travelled a great deal to places in the UK for leisure and I went on many a good conference for my work at the University of Hull. I loved it! I remember when I went to a conference in Dublin, at Trinity College, all expenses paid. It was superb. I thought how lucky I was. I went back to Dublin every year after that, always going to one of my favourite places on earth, Powerscourt Estate. I love sitting outside and having lunch overlooking Sugarloaf mountain.

When I was about 36, I decided to research my family tree on my mother's side of the family, as I found hers the most interesting, she having been born in Campbeltown. Her dad William Crossan had been brought up in Ramelton, County Donegal. I went there in about 1996 to see what it was like, and where he had been brought up. It is absolutely beautiful. I returned recently with my husband and it was wonderful to see it again. I feel so at home there. I can't explain it, but I do feel so at home in Ramelton and the surrounding areas. We stayed in Letterkenny, and I feel as if the people 'understand' me.

The first time I went I stayed at a small bed and breakfast in Ramelton and the landlady was lovely. Her husband had not long died and she seemed so sad. I had booked bed and breakfast, but on the evening she asked me if I would like to eat with her and watch the television, which was really nice. One day I had decided to travel to the Old Lammas Fair in Ballycastle, north of the border. At that time, the boat from Campbeltown used to cross to Ballycastle, so I thought I would like to go and see it.

On the day that I was travelling, I was supposed to catch a bus in the market place. I stood there waiting for the bus, and it didn't arrive. What I did see was a cream coloured bus with an orange stripe going all around it, disappear round a corner further down the street.

I went back to the boarding house to say the bus hadn't turned up, but that I had seen a bus further down. The landlady gave an exclamation and banged her forehead with the palm of her hand. 'Oh no, that's the new market place, I left you at the old market place, I'm so sorry.'

Anyway, she got a neighbour to take me to Letterkenny to see if I could catch another bus to Ballycastle, which I did. I thought it was very kind of the neighbour. They were all so helpful and friendly.

Once I got to Ballycastle it seemed so exciting and chaotic; there were hundreds of buses and we parked up and I went to look around. I went into a church just to cool down a bit as it was very hot, but decided to go back to where the bus was parked and see if I could see the cream bus with the orange stripe that I had missed earlier in the day. I knew it would be impossible with the hundreds of buses around, but I also just wanted to make sure I knew where the bus I had travelled on was parked.

I managed to find the bus I had travelled on and smiled to myself. Yes, I knew exactly where I was going, I could relax now and enjoy the fair. As I looked around, not for one minute thinking that I would see the bus I had missed earlier, I couldn't believe it, when two buses away from the bus I had travelled on that morning, was the bus I had missed, the cream bus with the orange stripe. There were two girls sitting on the grass verge next to the bus.

'Did you travel on this bus this morning?.'

'Yes,' they said.

'Did it come from Rathmullan and go through Ramelton?'

'Yes, they said.

'And what time is it going back tonight?

'Six o'clock,' they replied.

'Thank you.'

The bus I had travelled on was due to leave at six as well, so I could ask the bus driver if I could get a lift back all the way to Ramelton, instead of having to stop off at Letterkenny and get another bus. If I couldn't, then I could just get the bus I had travelled on.

I went back to the church to listen to some music and then I walked through all the stalls that lined the street. It was wonderful!

As I got to the sea front, I could see the sign that pointed the way to the ferry to Campbeltown. I went to lunch in the pub. I went back to the church in the afternoon for tea and I was telling a young man in the church all about my experience with the bus. The priest/vicar overheard my conversation and he said. 'That's fantastic,' but if you can't get the bus or you have any trouble getting on the buses, you come back here and I'll drive you back to Ramelton. We can't have you stranded.' I thought it was really great how kind the people were.

I went back to the bus just before six and spoke with both drivers. I managed to get a lift on the bus I had missed and get back to Ramelton without changing at Letterkenny. All was well. I just found it extraordinary that I found that bus amongst all those buses parked up, and that it was only two buses away from the one I had arrived on. Thank you for your goodness universe.

8

Changes

'The Lord is my light and my salvation; whom shall I fear? The Lord is the stronghold of my life, of whom shall I be afraid?' (Psalms 27.1).

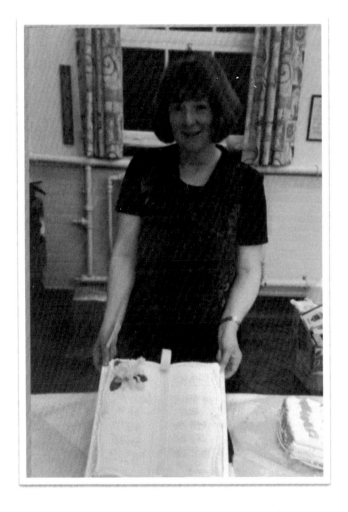

The beautiful cake made into a page of scripture for my 40th birthday

As far as I was aware my life was pretty much set in a pattern. I had been a Chartered Librarian for nearly 17 years and didn't expect that at my place of employment management decided to put pressure on me because I had become ill. In 2000 I developed BPPV, Benign Paroxysmal Positional Vertigo. The first time I experienced it was one Sunday morning at about 3am. I was sleeping and I woke up spinning in the bed. I thought the bed was moving, I started to vomit, I screamed out. 'What's happening?' It felt like there was a huge maleficent presence in the room. It was scary. I tried to ring my family, my mam and my brother. I couldn't remember the number, my hands and body were shaking all over. I crawled to the telephone. I eventually managed to ring my mam and brother and they advised me to ring a doctor, which I did. I left the door open so he could come in. When he did arrive not long after I rang, he just looked at me and said, 'oh vertigo, I thought it would be.' All very matter of factly. He placed a pill under my tongue and told me to go and see my doctor on Monday.

I was off work for three days after that first episode of vertigo, and then came many years of trying to find out what I had. At first I seemed to get the attacks once a year, which I could cope with, then it got to once a month and then daily. One day I could be perfectly well; then get a vertigo attack during the night, be off work the next day and return to work the following day. Apparently, according to my place of employment, that was the problem. They couldn't understand it. They certainly didn't understand and didn't even want to understand my illness/disability. People can be unbearably cruel when they don't understand something and I was treated very badly as a consequence.

I struggled with BPPV for over 7 years, when I realised I

couldn't live like that. Nearly every day I woke up I was sick with having a vertigo episode nearly every night, waking up being violently sick and unable to walk straight. From having attacks yearly, which I could cope with, it went to monthly, and then daily. I went to the doctor and said, 'I can't live like this anymore, it's affecting my whole life'. And because my place of employment were not sympathetic to me and caused more stress, it actually made matters worse with my illness, stress not helping it at all.

My doctor sent me to Hull Royal Infirmary Ear, Nose and Throat Department, where an amazing young man performed the Epley Manoeuvre on me. The Epley Manoeuvre meant that I sat on a table and was pulled back quickly to laying position with my head slightly over the edge of the table, first to the left and then to the right. I started spinning instantly and started screaming. 'You have it in this ear as well, did you realise?' I hadn't realised, it seemed to be coming from my left ear, but as he looked intently at my eyes, he could see their fast movement. 'It's a persistent little thing.' He waited for my eyes to become still and then he turned me quickly to the left side. I started screaming again, as the room spun and spun around and I felt so sick.

I was trying to get up because, as I had discovered from experience, if you get up quickly and keep your head still and straight, you can have a certain amount of control over the spinning, but the young man held me down. 'I'm sorry,' he said, 'You'll ruin the effects of this if you move now.' The spinning slowly subsided. Then he turned me around on my front. Again the room started spinning. 'I know you may not believe this, but this is actually doing you good.' He said. There had been another young apprentice in the room watching the whole procedure. He was fascinated. 'Wow,' he said, 'I've never seen anything like it.'

Once the procedure had finished, I got up very slowly as I was totally disorientated. The last instructions from the young man was that when I went to bed for the next two evenings, I should sleep sitting up. It was difficult to do, but well worth it.

Thanks to that young man, I have been almost totally free from BPPV for years. I still get it if I do things like lowering my head to look under something, i.e. a desk or table, or if I get on the floor to do exercises. That is always difficult. Sometimes, as well, I still wake up with a start as the room starts to spin around. Certainly though, I don't get it as bad as I did, and for that I am eternally grateful to the young man. It all came to a head at work when my mam died on July 18th 2007 at the age of 85, she would have been 86 on the August 30th 2007.

I had handed my notice in because I couldn't take anymore of what was happening. I think it was something like 2 months notice (not sure now, but it was quite a long time). I was sitting having coffee in the sunshine on Tuesday 10th July 2007. I rang my sister to see how my mam was, because she had been acting strange when I had gone round there on the Sunday. When I looked at her, her eyes looked different. I even said to my brother, 'do you think Mam has had a little stroke.' When I rang my sister she was concerned that mam wasn't right, but she had to leave her to get back for her family. I decided there and then to go and see my Mam. I went back to my office and explained that I would be leaving to see if my mam was ok and I got a lift from a friend at the time. It was the last time I ever saw my office. I never went back to that job.

I was given time off by the doctor to see my mam every day

at the hospital. I was with her when she died, and although I didn't want to lose my best friend, if you have to die, which we all do, I would like to die peacefully like my mam. I held her hand and told her I loved her and I told her we all loved her.

A few years before my mam died, she started to feel the cold a lot. Even if it was a beautiful sunny day, she always had large woollen cardigans on her. Because she felt the cold, she thought everyone else felt the cold as well. When we went into her house, the heat was the first thing that hit you. It was so hot. When we went out of the house she would say, 'Where's your coat? Put your coat on.' We would say, 'Mother, it's a glorious day outside. It's not cold.' She would say, 'Oh, I'm freezing.'

Two weeks' after my mam's death, I was in St Charles church to light a candle. I go in there quite often as it is peaceful and away from the noise and bustle of the city. It was a lovely, sunny day outside and I was wearing a dress with a short sleeved summer jacket. As I entered the church I could see there was only one woman in. I went to make my way to the candle stand and the woman approached me with a reprimand, 'Where's your coat?' She asked. 'Sorry,' I said, wondering why a complete stranger had come up to me and asked 'Where's your coat?' the very same question my mam would have asked. The woman looked at me as if she were in total shock. 'I'm so sorry, I don't know why I said that.' The woman was so distressed and embarrassed, she kept apologising. It was as if she had suddenly come to her senses.

I lit the candle and sat in the church trying to work out what had just happened. Was that my mam trying to tell me she was ok. Trying to tell me everything was alright and that there is a life after death? That we move on? I just don't know. I have a faith, but for the first time, it was confirmed to me that there is life after death. I have heard stories from people about their loved ones when they have died as well, such as clocks starting up again that haven't worked for years, and it belonged to the person who had died.

I was off work until the end of my notice, so I never returned to that job. I didn't know how I would live without my mam, but being with her when she died, somehow gave me a great strength and the incident in the church made me believe that she was fine and she still looked out for me. She was such a lovely person. She used to sit in her chair and watch the television. She loved to read, but in later years her eyesight deteriorated and she couldn't, so the television was her only entertainment. She loved the adverts, and there was an advert with a frog on it to the tune of Day Dream Believer by the Monkees. I used to watch her face when she watched this. She laughed and laughed. She loved it. I laughed at her laughing. After she died, it seemed whenever I was down, Day Dream Believer played on the radio. Again, it seemed as if she were saying, 'Everything is fine. Everything will be alright. And that is what Mam always used to say to me, 'Everything will be alright love.'

I didn't think I would ever laugh again after my mam died and losing my job. What on earth would I do? I kept hearing my mam's voice say, 'It'll be alright, love.'

I thought I would totally crumble when I lost my mam, but there was something about seeing her die; being with her, and knowing she had died peacefully, made me strong and I always felt her love. There is not a day goes by when I don't think of her.

Two years after her death, I had been to work and gone into

town straight from work to do some clothes shopping. It was late opening on a Thursday evening.

When my mam had been alive, we spoke to each other every day; ringing each other at 9pm.

When I got home from my shopping trip, I fell asleep on the settee. In my dream, I had been speaking with my mam. We had been in town with each other and as we said goodbye, she said, 'I'll ring you when you get home.'

The next thing the telephone rang and I got up from the settee and looked at the clock. It was 9pm and it confirmed to me that it would be Mam on the other end of the telephone,

I answered, 'Hello.'

'Hi, Pete here.'

'Oh,' I said, 'I thought it was Mam, she said she'd ring me when I got home from town.'

My brother said, 'Patricia, are you alright?'

Apparently, my brother had said this at least three times, because I kept saying, 'I thought it was Mam, she said she would ring when I got home.'

Suddenly, I could feel myself coming completely out of my sleep. 'Oh, what am I saying? Mam died.' Then I felt silly. 'Oh just ignore me, I'm still half asleep and I had a dream that I was in town with Mam and she said she would ring me when I got home.'

Peter was relieved when I had come to. He thought I was having a stroke. He said if I hadn't come out of it, he was going to come round to the flat to make sure I was alright. What a coincidence though that I had that dream that mam was going to ring me, and the phone rang at 9pm, the exact time she would have rang me.

Me and Mam on holiday at Scarborough

The incident actually highlighted something that had been happening to me for years. Strange things happened – for example, once, I looked at my left arm one night and it had a huge white triangle, circle and square on it. I kept trying to rub it away and it wouldn't go. I couldn't make head nor tail of it. Eventually, it faded away, but left me puzzled for years. Another time, I had been Thursday night shopping and bought a light blue summer jacket. It was spotless. I hung it in the bedroom. When I went back to look at it, there was a huge stain on the front of it. Not just a stain when I felt it, it felt as if it were totally ingrained and hard. I couldn't believe it. How had I not noticed that? I even rang the shop and told them that I was going to take it back. After I rang the shop, I went back to look at the jacket again, and the stain had gone. I felt the part where the stain had been, and it wasn't there. It wasn't hard, it was soft and blue again. The stain had totally vanished. What?

After the incident with my brother ringing up and I was saying I was waiting for my mam to ring, then realising that I was still half asleep after having a nap on the settee; I realised that the connection between all these events was that I had been sleeping beforehand. Although I was moving about and talking, I was still half asleep, I was very relieved by this, as I thought I was going mad. Mystery solved.

I did laugh again. In the September of 2007, I got a job at the Hull Daily Mail as a website moderator on 'this is YourMail.' I was there for just over a year, but it was a terrific year. I loved every minute of it. I had always wanted to work at the Hull Daily Mail, ever since I was young. I remember the day of the interview. I hadn't wanted to go, as I was still grieving for the loss of my mam, and it didn't seem important; but I dressed up and went with my new bag, which was spotted straight away by one of the interviewers. 'I love your bag,' she said. That broke the ice. It was a lovely interview, very special and I thought that I got the job, but I hadn't heard anything for over a week. I really wanted that job, so I rang up to check. The secretary there was shocked. 'Of course you got the job, oh for goodness sake, didn't Alex ring you? I'm just typing up the letter now, so you'll get that soon.'

I was so relieved. I was working with two other people.

They were young and vibrant and made me laugh so much. We did so many exciting things. It was such good fun to work for the Hull Daily Mail. The team I was in had their own patch and went out to meet people. There was many a time we would have morning coffee at a local café in the centre of town and meet people who had used the website, to get their thoughts on the website.

We also went to local schools to give a talk and invited schools in to see what we did.

It's a shame the YourMail website was short lived, but it was good while it lasted and I realised that I could laugh again.

The Website won many awards.

I went to an awards ceremony where we didn't win for the website that time, but we did win in other areas. It was a very exciting world at the Hull Daily Mail, and I'm so pleased I had the opportunity of working there.

9

I Love a Good Wedding

'To see your face in a crowd of others, or alone on a frightening street. I weep for that.' (Rumi).

I was just four years old when I was bridesmaid for the first time at my oldest sisters wedding. The wedding was at St. Theresa's Church on Longhill Estate. I remember it very clearly, even though I was only four years old. I seemed to be on show, in my beautiful white dress, headdress of white flowers and silver shoes. Oh how I loved those silver shoes. I wore them until they fell off my feet. I wore them everywhere, much to my mother's embarrassment. I wore them to bed and she had to take them off me when I was asleep. In the end she just had to throw them away, because they were in tatters, I had worn them that much. I was most upset. Even though she bought me a new pair of silver shoes, they weren't the same, and I didn't wear those new shoes. Even to this day, I love my bling and as I sit here in the sunshine in the garden, writing this book, I'm wearing beautiful shiny, rose gold and silver shoes. I've worn them for weeks and will continue to do so until they fall off my feet. (They have now become my gardening shoes).

There is a photograph of me as a bridesmaid, standing on the steps. The look on my face says it all. I didn't like being the centre of attention, and I remember the feelings standing on the stairs. 'What was everyone looking at?' I couldn't smile. I'd never experienced anything like this before. What was it?

Me as a bridesmaid at my sister Cath's wedding

I was eight years old when I was the bridesmaid at my second sisters wedding. I was a little bit on the podgy side. I remember there was quite a fuss about me being overweight, but when I look back at the photograph, I was a healthy, growing girl and I looked beautiful. Yet, I was made to feel awful. I thought there was something wrong with me. They needn't have worried because I went incredibly slim not long after, so much so, they were worried I had anorexia. You can't win.

During the years of eight to eleven, I was plump. I remember it seemed to be a big deal, but looking back at photographs, I think people were making too big a fuss about it. I was growing, I looked healthy and actually was not too fat at all, not as fat as the adults made me feel, and self-conscious about my looks. They shouldn't have worried, because I went very thin at the age of 14 and continued to be thin throughout my years until the age of 50 (that is another story).

I was 15 when I was bridesmaid at my third sister's wedding. I was thin and felt great.

My sister and all the bridesmaids had their hair done in Hammonds on the morning of the wedding. My brother came to see if he could find us, because he had seen Sparks in the town centre. As it happened they were playing at the University of Hull on the day of my sister's wedding. I didn't see them that day, but I saw them in Torquay the week after.

My sister Linda's wedding. I am on the far right.

There is a saying, 'Three times bridesmaid, never a blushing bride…' I became a bride, even though it had taken a long time. I was 52 when I married.

At 52, I just wanted a fairly quiet marriage with family and friends around me to share the moment and have a meal together. That's why the Kingston Theatre Hotel was a wonderful place to have our wedding. It was handled very well by the team. I felt that at my age, I didn't want anything elaborate or to wear anything over the top, although I ended up wearing something I didn't really want to wear.

I had looked and looked for a wedding dress. The cheapest one was actually a bridesmaid dress, but I wanted to be the bride, so I went to get a wedding dress. Because I was quite large at the time and it was very difficult to find a dress to fit me. I found a dress for £100 on the internet, but what I didn't realise was that as it was being sent from abroad, I had to pay £70 to get it released from the airport. Then, when it arrived, it was actually too big. I had to pay another £90 to get it taken in. So my £100 dress cost £260 in the end. When I look at the lovely photograph my husband's brother took of us just at the end of the wedding ceremony, I feel that I actually do like it and I'm pleased with it. I hadn't seen it fully until I saw that photograph.

The Kingston Theatre Hotel was once the home of Madame Clapham, dressmaker to royalty.

I stayed at the hotel the night before my wedding and hung my wedding dress up. I realised that the hem and the lace at the bottom of the dress were coming apart, and I spent some of the night sewing it up. I think Madame Clapham would have been very pleased with me sewing my hem up on the dress. Her spirit was certainly to be felt. Fifty people, family and friends were at our wedding. All I wanted on the day were those close to me and those I love and those who love me, to share a meal together and celebrate my marriage to Allan. It was a beautiful day.

My husband and I travelled first-class to Kirkcaldy the following Tuesday after the wedding. I think that was my honeymoon. Then came the arduous task of trying to find a job.

My wedding was very sweet. All fifty guests showed up and we had a sit down meal. Because of my age, I wanted something very simple and not over the top. I thought that was for young couples, but actually, I think you should be able to have what you want at any age. We had originally said that we would go to the register office in Kirkcaldy, just the two of us, but then when family heard, they wanted to be at the wedding, so we decided to make it a small affair of fifty guests, and just the wedding, not an evening do as well. I'm not a party person.

What was lovely, was the fact that I had all the people there that I wanted to be there and I felt the love in the room, and as someone said to me, 'everyone at your wedding loves you.'

The music I walked in to was Amici Forever singing Whisper of Angels. It was so beautiful. And although people may think the words are about my love for Allan (which it is as well), it is really about mine and Allan's love for God and how we belong to Him and have done so since the beginning of time and forever more.

Even though I didn't have a church wedding, it was very much a spiritual and heavenly wedding, with every little detail relating to God. He is the centre of our lives.

Once I married, I instantly became a mother and grandmother to Allan's two daughters and granddaughter. Although his daughters didn't need me to be a mother, it is lovely to be called 'grandma,' a word I didn't think I would be called.

Mr and Mrs Levack, Kingston Theatre Hotel,
November 16th 2012

My words to Allan and Allan's words to me, come from Rumi:

The Most Alive Moment
'The most alive moment comes
when those who love each other

114

meet each other's eyes
and in what flows between them then.

To see your face in a crowd of others,
or alone on a frightening street,
I weep for that.
Our tears improve the earth.
The things you taught me,
your gratitude, your laughing,
always your qualities increase the soul.

Seeing you is a wine
that does not muddle or numb.

We sit inside the cypress shadow
where amazement and clear thought
twine their slow growth into us.'

And when we exchanged rings, I said to Allan:-

'I take you to be my husband for life.
I promise to live in truth and love with you.
And to communicate fully in love and understanding.
I give you my hand and my heart as a sanctuary of warmth
and peace.
And I pledge my love and devotion to you on our journey
through life together.'

Allan's words to me:

This Marriage
(Rumi's ode 2667)
'May these vows and this marriage be blessed.
May it be sweet milk, this marriage,
Like wine and halvah.
May this marriage offer fruit and shade
Like the date palm.
May this marriage be full of laughter,
Our every day a day in paradise.
May this marriage have a fair face and a good name,
An omen as welcome as the moon in a clear blue sky.
I am out of words to describe how spirit mingles in this marriage.'
Both are by Mevlana Jalaluddin Rumi tr by Kabir Helminski.

And Allan's words to me after we had exchanged rings:
'On this day,
I give you my heart,
My promise,
That I will walk with you,
Hand in hand,
Wherever our journey leads us,
Living, learning, loving,
Together,
Forever.'

10

The City of Hull: Past and Present

'For Hull has its own sudden elegancies.' (Philip Larkin).

I love Hull and I enjoyed my younger days growing up there. We did so much as youngsters in the school holidays, roaming around the local area, and then going into town at the weekends. The local parks were our playground.

The places I remember as a young girl were the areas around where I used to live. It was a small world, but a good world to me, it consisted of my house, the neighbours' houses, parks, big shops, little shops and a lot of visits to the doctor on Holderness Road. I seemed to be at the doctor a lot when I was little and always seemed to have some sort of illness, including mumps, measles, chicken pox; all the usual childhood diseases.

It was very rare that I went into town when I was younger, and when I started primary school, my world expanded a bit as I travelled by bus to the school and visited friends homes, that were a bit further afield than my immediate neighbours' houses. My world began to expand.

Hull FC and Hull Kingston Rovers.

I don't know much about football, but there seemed to be a divide within the City of Hull. When Hull FC and Hull KR played at Wembley in 1980, there was Wembley fever everywhere. My brother-in-law and his brother went to watch them, and Rovers won 10-5.

I was walking down the street on the day and a young boy of about four or five, had a rock in his hand, ready to throw. 'Who do you support, Hull FC or Rovers?'

My heart sank. He was only little, but a rock like that would hurt if thrown.

'No-one,' I said and just walked straight past, my heart beating madly.

His little mind obviously wasn't ready for that reply and he put the rock down, much to my relief.

I don't really know that much about rugby or football – it was never a part of my family life, but I was working at the Hull Daily Mail in 2008 on the YourMail Website when Tigers went to Wembley – what excitement.

Dean Windass volleyed Hull City into the Premier League for the first time in the club's 104-year history. The 39-year-old striker's spectacular first-half shot from 18 yards was enough to beat Bristol City in the Championship play-off final at Wembley.

It was a moment of triumph for Hull boss Phil Brown and his players, but it was the veteran Windass who was to claim the glory after hitting the winner on his first appearance at Wembley in a long and distinguished career.

Hull Fair

Hull Fair started in the year 1278 and it is still is a big event in Hull. Certainly, when I was young, we looked forward to it coming to town. It had the carousel, slides, candyfloss, dolls on sticks, fish you could win and all manner of peculiar side-shows; the bearded lady, shrunken heads, Siamese twins in a bottle; all frowned upon today.

I went to the fair with family up to the age of 14 and then with friends.

I stopped going when I was about 15 and then one last time in my thirties. It had changed beyond all recognition. The side-shows of old had long been replaced. I suppose they were outdated and not very pc. I found it very crowded and I don't like crowds at all. Dad, I think, loved going to Hull Fair.

It was exciting, the noise, the smells, the music, the excitement of seeing people screaming on the ever elaborate machines. It seemed to be colourful and magical everywhere I looked, when I was younger.

I didn't go on the roundabouts as I tended to get sick. Anything that went around and around was not good for me, but I could go on the carousel and the slide. That was about it, until I went with friends and I went on a terrifying machine, I can't remember the name, that flung me around in the air. Shaped like a bomb, I went straight into the sky, and then dive bombed to earth. I can still hear my screams and the fear I felt. Are we mad, putting ourselves through such fear?

I used to love coming home with candy floss, brandy snap and when I was very young, a doll on a stick. The atmosphere was electric, the music and smells, the people.

I haven't been to Hull Fair for years, but I know people who come back to Hull every year for the Fair no matter where they are in the world.

Three Ships Mosaic

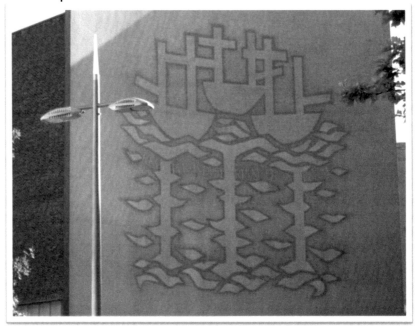

Artwork above what used to be BHS
– the painting spells out Hull

Of all the years passing this mosaic of the 'Three Ships' situated above what used to house the BHS shop, it was only in 2016 that I realised it spelt out Hull in the ships masts. How crazy is that?

The sculptor of this mosaic, Alan Boyson, died in 2018 aged 88.

The mosaic was originally commissioned by the Co-operative Society for their new department store in 1963, but I can only ever remember the BHS Store on this site.

'The mosaic is composed of 4,224 foot square slabs each made up of 225 tiny cubes of coloured Italian glass.' (Hull Daily Mail, 28th August 2018).

There is a sentence in Latin on the mural which says res per industriam prosperae, which means 'the success of industry.' It still remains to be seen what they will do with the mosaic now that the BHS Store is no longer there. There is talk of redevelopment of this site, but it is still not sure what will happen to the mosaic.

I for one, hope it stays in the town centre, somewhere.

The Deep Aquarium

The Deep aquarium is reckoned to be the world's only submarium - meaning it's partly submerged in the water that surrounds it. It's home to over 3,500 fish including Europe's only pair of green sawfish.

It is also home to sharks, rays and loads of other types of ocean living creatures. One of the displays at The Deep has 2.5 million litres of water with 87 tonnes of salt in it, to make it feel just like home for the fish inside.

The Deep

I return to Hull whenever I get the opportunity. I love it so much. My family live in Hull, sisters, brothers, nieces and nephews and I have remained friends with many other people.

Hull has changed a lot from when I was young, but Hull isn't unique in this. Community never stands still anywhere, as this has been proved throughout history.

My husband and I return to all our favourite places: Places we can't miss when we visit Hull. We love the town centre and will sit for ages at cafes that have outside tables and we watch the world go by.

Philip Larkin

In 1982, Larkin wrote a foreword to an anthology of works by local poets. He wrote: 'Hull has its own sudden elegancies. People are slow to leave it, quick to return. And there are others who come, as they think, for a year or two, and stay a lifetime, sensing that they have found a city that is in the world yet sufficiently on the edge of it to have a different resonance.'

Me with the statue of Philip Larkin at the Hull Interchange, Paragon Station

Philip Larkin died in 1985 in Hull; 5 years before I started work at the university of Hull Brynmor Jones Library, where Philip Larkin was Librarian.

From day one, I heard many stories about Philip Larkin and people were obviously inspired and in awe of him. I liked the sound of his interview style. As one colleague told me, 'He said, as long as they looked clean and presentable, I gave them the job.'

The statue of him at the Hull Interchange is larger than life, and by all accounts, he was larger than life and very charismatic. Although he wasn't born in Hull, the Hull people seemed to take him to their hearts. We now have something called, 'The Larkin Trail' which shows where Larkin was at his happiest in Hull.

Hull also produced the Toads, from Larkin's poem 'Toads Revisited.' 'Give me your arm old toad, and help me down Cemetery Road.'

The toads were placed around Hull for a while and then sold off for charity.

Truelove

TrueLove, Memiadluk and Uckaluk

The two disembodied heads sit atop the barrier at the approach to the tidal surge barrier on the west side of the River Hull. They are by Stefan Gec (2002). According to a nearby plaque: 'In 1847 Memiadluk and Uckaluk arrived in Hull close to this site aboard the Truelove, a local whaling ship. The following year the married couple set sail for their home in Cumberland Sound, Baffin Island. During this journey Uckaluk died following an outbreak of measles on board the ship.' (Wikipedia).

They are quite haunting to see if you don't know that they are there, but it is quite moving to see them as well.

The Humber Bridge

'Although technically not in Hull, the Humber Bridge is a spectacular road into the city.

It is a single-span suspension bridge stretching an enormous 1.3 miles (2.2 kilometres) with towers 155.5 meters tall and 71,000 kilometres (44,000 miles) of cable supporting the road.

The road carries an average of 120,000 cars per week while it bends more than 3 metres in winds up to 134 kilometres per hour (80mph). In 2013, with the help of girl guides, Blue Peter's Helen Skelton broke a world record covering the full length of the bridge with bunting.' (Wikapedia)

I remember when the bridge was being built and the problems that they had with it, but it all worked out well and was opened by the Queen on July 17th 1981 when I had completed my first year at college. The bridge was open to traffic on June 24th 1981. There was great excitement around it at the time, but it meant an end to the ferry that went across from Hull to New Holland, and a lot of people weren't happy about that.

David Whitfield

David Whitfield Statue outside Hull New Theatre

'Whitfield was born in Hull in the East Riding of Yorkshire. He sang in the choir at his church during his childhood and entertained his fellow members of the Royal Navy during the Second World War. After the war, he appeared on Opportunity Knocks, a talent show on Radio Luxembourg. His first recording to reach the Top 10 of the UK Singles Chart was 'Bridge of Sighs'. 'Answer Me, Oh Lord' (later recorded with different lyrics as 'Answer Me, My Love') reached number one in the UK. Both versions have appeared on CD.

Whitfield had other hits in the 1950s, and was the most successful British male singer in America during that period. He used orchestras, including Stanley Black, Mantovani and the Roland Shaw Orchestra, as backing accompaniment.

He was the first British male vocalist to earn a gold disc and the third overall. He was the first to reach the Top Ten of the Billboard Top 100, and the first artist from Britain to sell over a million copies of a record in the US. All of his hits were released by the Decca record label in the UK. His only album to reach the UK Albums Chart was The World of David Whitfield, which reached Number 19.

His most popular recordings were:

'Cara Mia' – with Mantovani which earned him that gold disc and gave him his second Number One in the UK Singles Chart.

'Answer Me' – his first UK chart topper.

'My September Love'

'I'll Find You' – the theme music to the 1957 film, Sea Wife, starring Joan Collins and Richard Burton.

'William Tell' – the theme music to the TV series, The Adventures of William Tell.

'Cara Mia' spent ten weeks at the pole position in the UK, making it one of the biggest selling British records in the pre-rock days. That recording co-credits Mantovani and his Orchestra and Chorus. Whitfield appeared on The Ed Sullivan Show and the 1954 Royal Command Performance. He continued to perform regularly across the globe, while living in Hull.

Many of his singles were issued on LP and have been reissued in recent years on CD compilations under licence. There were three 45rpm EP specials (1959–60), one entitled 'The Good Old Songs' and the other two featuring numbers from

'Rose Marie' and 'The Desert Song,' two musical shows in which Whitfield toured. On leaving Decca he recorded two singles for HMV (1962–63). His last LP, made for Philips in 1975 and entitled 'Hey There! It's David Whitfield,' included his third recording of 'Cara Mia' (he had already recorded a stereo re-make for Decca in 1966 for an album entitled Great Songs for Young Lovers). Whitfield's last single was for Denman, a coupling of 'Land of Hope and Glory' and 'When You Lose the One You Love' (1977).

He died from a brain haemorrhage in Sydney, Australia, while on tour at the age of 54.

A statue in the memory of Whitfield was unveiled outside of the New Theatre in Hull on 31 August 2012, before the opening night of a show celebrating the life and music of Whitfield.' (Wikipedia).

William Wilberforce

William Wilberforce

'Wilberforce was a deeply religious English member of parliament and social reformer who was very influential in the abolition of the slave trade and eventually slavery itself in the British empire.

William Wilberforce was born on 24 August 1759 in Hull, the son of a wealthy merchant. He studied at Cambridge University where he began a lasting friendship with the future prime minister, William Pitt the Younger. In 1780, Wilberforce became member of parliament for Hull, later representing Yorkshire. His dissolute lifestyle changed completely when he became an evangelical Christian, and in 1790 joined a leading group known as the Clapham Sect. His Christian faith prompted him to become interested in social reform, particularly the improvement of factory conditions in Britain.

The abolitionist Thomas Clarkson had an enormous influence on Wilberforce. He and others were campaigning for an end to the trade in which British ships were carrying black slaves from Africa, in terrible conditions, to the West Indies as goods to be bought and sold. Wilberforce was persuaded to lobby for the abolition of the slave trade and for 18 years he regularly introduced anti-slavery motions in parliament. The campaign was supported by many members of the Clapham Sect and other abolitionists who raised public awareness of their cause with pamphlets, books, rallies and petitions. In 1807, the slave trade was finally abolished, but this did not free those who were already slaves. It was not until 1833 that an act was passed giving freedom to all slaves in the British empire.

Wilberforce's other efforts to 'renew society' included the organisation of the Society for the Suppression of Vice in 1802. He worked with the reformer, Hannah More, in the

Association for the Better Observance of Sunday. Its goal was to provide all children with regular education in reading, personal hygiene and religion. He was closely involved with the Royal Society for the Prevention of Cruelty to Animals. He was also instrumental in encouraging Christian missionaries to go to India.

Wilberforce retired from politics in 1825 and died on 29 July 1833, shortly after the act to free slaves in the British empire passed through the House of Commons. He was buried near his friend Pitt in Westminster Abbey.

Amazing Grace is a 2006 British-American biographical drama film directed by Michael Apted, about the campaign against slave trade in the British Empire, led by William Wilberforce, who was responsible for steering anti-slave trade legislation through the British parliament. The title is a reference to the hymn 'Amazing Grace'. The film also recounts the experiences of John Newton as a crewman on a slave ship and subsequent religious conversion, which inspired his writing of the poem later used in the hymn. Newton is portrayed as a major influence on Wilberforce and the abolition movement.

The film premiered on 16 September 2006 at the Toronto International Film Festival, followed by showings at the Heartland Film Festival, the Santa Barbara International Film Festival, and the European Film Market, before opening in wide US release on 23 February 2007, which coincided with the 200th anniversary of the date the British parliament voted to ban the slave trade.' (Wikipedia and bbc.co.uk).

Telephone Boxes in Hull

Telephone boxes in Hull

A strange fact about Hull is that telephone company BT have never run the public phone boxes in the city. All of the communications in the city were run by the city council until 2007 and so all of the phone boxes are white, not the usual red that BT uses. Some are decorated for special occasions.

My family didn't have a telephone until 1979 when we moved into our second house when I was 19. Prior to this we used a public telephone box on Welland Road, Longhill Estate. There was many a time there was a knock on our door to say that there was a telephone call for us. It was usually from my dad when he had been working away, and he wanted my mam to know when he was coming home. It amazes me now that people would go out of their way to come and let us know. It was very good of them. I believe that telephone box is still there to this day.

The Joke Shop

The joke shop in Hull is still there after all these years. As a child, we used to go there and buy such things as a whoopi cushion, plastic poo, cut finger and I'm sure lots of other things. I remember taking some things from the joke shop to school, but the fun didn't last long, because everyone had seen them before.

The Flower Clock – Freetown Way

I love the flower clock in Hull. Especially since I have taken up botanical illustration and art; I seem to have gone mad for anything relating to flowers. I have seen the flower clock in Hull at the head of Freetown Way for 12 years. It's something thousands of people pass a day and they either see it or they don't. I've asked many people about the flower clock and they have said they never knew it was there. But afterwards when they have been to town again, they realise that indeed, they have seen it. It's one of those comforting things that is always there and I hope it remains so.

My interpretation of the flower clock for 2017
City of Culture status

The Language of Flowers

This painting in watercolour and acrylic is based upon the flower clock situated at the junction of Freetown Way, Hull. I want to show the beauty and diversity of Hull by using the language of flowers. The flowers on the clock represent the communities living in Hull.

There are twenty one National Flowers on the clock and the first flower to be grown on the International Space Station, the Zinnia – I put this flower in to represent the Universality of Man, and because, inevitably, I haven't been able to include all the National Flowers on the painting due to space, and many countries don't have a national flower.

1 o'clock

Tulip – Hungary, Netherlands, Turkey

Cherry blossom – Japan

2 o'clock

Thistle – Scotland

Peony – China

3 o'clock

Daffodil – Wales

Flax – Belarus

4 o'clock

Rose – England, America, Bulgaria

Shamrock – Ireland

Space Flower – Universal Man

5 o'clock

Daisy – Italy, Latvia

6 o'clock

Dog Rose – Romania

7 o'clock

Jasmine – Syria, Pakistan

8 o'clock

Rue – Lithuania
Iris – France
Lotus Flower – India, Vietnam
9 o'clock
Cornflower – Prussia, Estonia, Germany
Poppy – Belgium
10 o'clock
Carnation – Spain, Monaco
Sunflower – Ukraine
11 o'clock
Passion Flower – Freetown, Sierra Leone
12 o'clock
Pansy – Poland

At the centre of my flower clock is the Yorkshire Rose surrounded by Ivy representing vitality in friendships and honouring differences, not just enjoying similarities.

The hands of the clock are set to 2017.

This painting is to celebrate the gardeners of Hull's parks and gardens, who work so hard to keep Hull looking so beautiful; and to celebrate the communities of Hull that make Hull vibrant and diverse.

The flower clock was installed in its current position on Freetown Way in 2005. Thanks to Simon Race, Horticultural Officer, who draws up schemes for the clock and chooses the type and variety of plants to use; and to all the people who help maintain the flower clock.

The Gardener
By Andrew Marvell. Publ. 1681
'How well the skilful gard'ner drew
of flow'rs and herbs this dial new,
Where from above the milder sun
Does through a fragrant zodiac run;

And as it works, th' industrious bee
Computes its time as well as we.
How could such sweet and wholesome hour
Be reckoned but with herbs and flower.'

Part Two:
Living in Scotland

'Light in Scotland has a quality I have not met elsewhere. It is luminous without being fierce, penetrating to immense distances with an effortless intensity.' (Nan Shepherd, The Living Mountain).

Watercolour painting by Tricia Levack

11

The Chisholme Institute
Beshara School of Esoteric Education

'The people of Perfection are they who, paying attention to their breathing, become like guardians to the Treasury of their hearts. Let them stand there as guardian and do not allow any stranger to enter. The Treasury of the Heart is the Library of God. Let him not allow thoughts other than those concerning God to enter.' (Ibn Arabi, Kernel of the Kernel).

The Chisholme Institute, Roberton, Hawick, Scotland

Scotland has always been a part of my life. As I said before, my mam was born in Campbeltown on the west coast of Scotland, and I travelled there when I was young. I traced my ancestry back to 1715 in that part of Scotland.

I gave up everything when my mam died in 2007. I had always wanted to take the second six month residential course at the Chisholme Institute on the borders of Scotland. I had taken the first course in October 1986 to March 1987 and it had changed my life. I didn't think I would ever get the opportunity to do the second course as it was too expensive for me. But I asked and prayed to do it from 2007. I went for a week to Chisholme again after my mam died and I knew then that I had to do the second course. I didn't know how; how would I pay for it? I had no idea. I just knew that I had to do it.

I didn't know if I would be able to stay in one place for 6 months. I like my own space and people can be on top of each other sometimes at Chisholme. So I decided to go for one week and study there to see if I would like it. I went for a week's study on 4th July 2010; the second course starting in October that same year.

Every time I have been to Chisholme, travelling up from Hull I have always seen rainbows. This journey was no exception. I arrived at Chisholme at 4pm in time for tea. I arrived in a taxi and there was a man sitting outside on a log, smoking. He came to greet me and I introduced myself and he introduced himself. Little did I know then, that he was going to be my husband, but looking back, it was just as if he had been sitting there waiting for me.

The Chisholme Institute, has been such an important part of my life. It is situated in Roberton, Hawick in its own grounds. I first went here in the year 1984 and then took a six month residential course here 1986-1987 and taking the second course 2010-2011, where I met my husband.

As I said in a previous chapter, I first heard of Chisholme when I was a student at Hull College of Higher Education. I watched 'Turning' about the dervishes and Turkey and Sufism. It was fascinating. I had seen the film before on one of my days playing truant and here it was again, on my course of religious studies.

The tutor on the course at Hull College was a director of the Chisholme Institute and invited students to attend the school; then called the Beshara School of Intensive Esoteric Education. The school had been running since 1975, with people from all over the world attending. It was a very exciting and vibrant place. Suddenly, I came in touch with people who felt the same way as me about life. Here I was, the little, uneducated person from a council estate, thinking and feeling the same as princes, aristocrats and people who came from all over the world, from all walks of life. It was different and unusual to my life in many ways, and in other ways, I felt very much at home at Chisholme.

Bulent Rauf was the spiritual director at the Chisholme Institute, a very charismatic man. Bulent was born in Istanbul in 1911 and died at Chisholme House in 1987, the year in which I completed my first course. I am so pleased too that he was there physically whilst I was at Chisholme. His presence was comforting and still is, comforting. His teachings were on 'the one Absolute Unity of all existence.' (tawhid).

'Bulent Rauf was the grandson of Ismail Pasha, Vice-regent of Egypt, the family having close connections to the Ottoman imperial house. He was educated first at home, where he had a classical Ottoman education, reading Turkish, Arabic and Persian as well as three European languages, and then continued his studies at Roberts College.

He attended Cornell and Yale Universities, and travelled widely. Then in 1945 he married his second cousin, Princess Faiza of Egypt. They were divorced in the early sixties. He settled in England in 1966 and married Angela Culme-Seymour.' (besharapublications.org.uk).

I didn't know this about Bulent when I went to Chisholme, I only knew straight away that he was an incredible man.

'What is the single most important point that must be understood by a person who wants to know?' Bulent asks in Addresses II.

'It is that there is only One, Unique, Absolute, Infinite Existence. It must be more than an idea. One has to be so completely certain of it that one adopts it through reason and intuition as the basic unshakeable fact of one's existence. When it is like that in one's existence, then every possible ramification that occurs to one is seen as not being outside the Existence, but as being an aspect of it. Accept and completely adopt the idea that there is only the Unique, Absolute Existence, apart from which there is not. Then constantly, or as much as possible, keep it in mind. Then, as only He can adopt such an idea, you disappear in the face of the awareness of this idea (which is Him in any case – who else could think of it?) Then your consciousness of this idea is your consciousness of His Existence: His Consciousness of Himself. Then where are you? You never were. He shows you He is yourself, then bit by bit He shows you how He is all that there is. These showings are His Caprices, until all exterior existence is known as Him. He shows you He is you, then shows you (Himself) that all else is Him. In the instant, all so-called progress is annihilated in Him.'

On the first six month course, I didn't see Bulent much, but when I did, there was always a lesson to be learned. I did have a 'thing' about not having money and seeing 'everyone' else enjoying themselves and seeming to be 'rich'. Bulent had joined the group for a meal and was sitting at the head of the table. Someone had come to kneel beside him to talk to him and Bulent had his back to me. I looked at him and was saying in my mind, 'It's alright for you though Bulent isn't it, you have money, you are well looked after.' With that thought, Bulent stopped talking to the man kneeling beside him and turned quickly and stared at me, with a look that challenged me. I realised he had read my mind and I returned to eating my soup and feeling thoroughly ashamed. What had I learned from this? There is more to life than meets the eye? I was incorrect in my views on money, poverty and riches? I'm really not sure what this meant, but I was put in my place. Bulent was indeed an extraordinary man. It was my perception that he had read my mind, I don't know, but I do know that Bulent was always aware of what was happening. Being in constancy of awareness was his message to the students.

In December 1986, I took my first trip abroad to Turkey, as part of the intensive esoteric course. This trip to Turkey, as we were reminded in a letter, was not a holiday, but a time for direction and devotion and pleading for the beneficence and himmah from the Source of All Himmah so that the intensive course could find its proper function and focus: that of advance towards, and approach to a state of non-being in Union (tawhid). (Himmah=spiritual assistance).

'Only he who has the love of tawhid branded in his heart brings light to the tomb of Ismail Hakki Bursevi.'

I loved the tomb of Ismail Hakki Bursevi, which is situated in

Bursa. He was a 17th-century Ottoman Turkish scholar, poet and musical composer.

We also visited places such as The Green Mosque in Bursa and The Blue Mosque and the Chora in Istanbul. I was stunned by their magnificence and beauty.

It was amazing. I had flown in a plane before, but this was the first time I went abroad. We first went to Istanbul, then toured all around Turkey, Ephesus, Bursa. We were in Konya for December 17th to watch the Whirling Dervishes; the order of Sufism practised by Rumi, and to see Rumi's tomb. Jelaluddin Rumi was a judge, teacher and poet.

I have been fascinated by Rumi, he was such an incredible man.

December 17th is a well-known date in Turkey. 'It commemorates the departure for eternal life of the one who, all his life, aspired toward the supreme meeting.' I just love this description of Rumi's funeral, told by Aflaki.

'After they had brought the corpse on a shaft, the totality of the people, rich and poor alike, uncovered their heads. Women, men and children, everyone was there. There was an uproar so loud that it could have been the day of the great Resurrection. Everyone was crying and most of the men were walking and wailing, tearing their robes, their bodies bare. The members of all communities and cultures were present, Christians, Jews, Greeks, Arabs, Turks etc. They walked in front, each holding high their Holy Book. Each was reading the Psalms, the Pentateuch or the Gospels, according to their faith. The hurling and lamenting was so great that the Moslems could not have held them back with canes or swords. The thunderous tumult was soon heard by the sultan and his minister Pervane who sent for the leaders of these denominations and asked them why they were so affected when the one they were mourning was the imam of the Moslems. They answered: 'When we saw him, we understood the real nature of Christ, of Moses and of all the prophets. We have found in him, the perfect conduct described in our Books as being the conduct of the perfect prophets. Just as you Moslems claim that Mawlana was the Mohammad of our time, so we think that is the Moses and the Jesus of our time, and just as you are his faithful friends, so are we, and a thousand times more, his servants and disciples.' (Rumi and Sufism).

This is so obviously a man who was well loved.

This trip to Turkey for me was the most enlightening. I thought I had been given a great gift. I could not have afforded to go, but because I was not working and not claiming any benefits of any kind; I received a cheque for over £300 which was tax owed to me. The cheque arrived about five weeks before I went to Turkey – just in time to be able to join the trip.

The first hotel we stayed in was the Pera Palas Hotel, where Agatha Christie had stayed. I thought I had died and gone to heaven. As I walked into the entrance hall I gasped at its beauty. I had never in my life stayed at such a beautiful hotel. We travelled all around Turkey. It was the most exciting thing I had ever done. It was another world; different sights, sounds and smells; everything massaging the senses. My eyes were wide with wonder.

We walked in a living history, visiting Ephesus and Mary's House, and Iznik, which was once called Nicea, where they held the First Council and discussed the qualities of God which resulted in the Nicene Creed (A.D.325).

The Nicene Creed

'We believe in one God, the Father, the Almighty, maker of

heaven and earth, of all that is, seen and unseen.

We believe in one Lord, Jesus Christ, the only Son of God, eternally begotten of the Father, God from God, Light from Light, true God from true God, begotten, not made, of one Being with the Father. Through him all things were made. For us and for our salvation he came down from heaven: by the power of the Holy Spirit he became incarnate from the Virgin Mary, and was made man. For our sake he was crucified under Pontius Pilate; he suffered death and was buried. On the third day he rose again in accordance with the Scriptures; he ascended into heaven and is seated at the right hand of the Father. He will come again in glory to judge the living and the dead, and his kingdom will have no end.

We believe in the Holy Spirit, the Lord, the giver of life, who proceeds from the Father. With the Father and the Son he is worshiped and glorified. He has spoken through the Prophets. We believe in one holy catholic and apostolic Church. We acknowledge one baptism for the forgiveness of sins. We look for the resurrection of the dead, and the life of the world to come. Amen.'

Note: The word 'catholic' with a lower case 'c' does not mean the Roman Catholic Church, but the universal Christian Church as a whole.

Travelling through Turkey brought the bible and history to life. I had read about Ephesus in the Bible. 'The first Christian community in Ephesus was established by St John and developed by St Paul. Paul came into the city to fulfill the promise that he had given on his brief visit when returning from Corinth and stayed for about three and a half years and also wrote his letters to Ephesians in captivity in Ephesus. When Paul came to Ephesus, he preached the gospel and gained followers. The church of Ephesus which became the head of the Seven Churches in western Asia Minor was established by Paul. He had a daily struggle with magicians and soothsayers in Ephesus while struggling with state offices and pagans. In a short time, Ephesus became the third important city of Christianity after Jerusalem and Antioch. Christianity rapidly gained popularity in Ephesus and by the popularity of this new religion, the jeweler Demetrius and others who earned a living by selling and making silver statues of Mother Goddess Artemis, were quite distressed. Demetrius and his colleagues provoked thousands of people and met with them in the Ephesus theatre and started shouting 'Great is Artemis of the Ephesians.' Paul wanted to face the crowd but disciples would not let him. Finally, the city clerk announced that the courts were open for people who had a complaint and dispersed the crowd. After this event St Paul left Ephesus and went to Macedonia. It is seen that Ephesus had an important place in the lives of both apostles John and Paul, but both of them were not in Ephesus at the same time. John and Paul led different communities in Ephesus.' (http://www.ephesus.us/ephesus/st_paul_in_ephesus.htm).

Standing in the ampitheatre at Ephesus, I could hear the ghosts of thousands of citizens of the past shouting, 'Great is Artemis of the Ephesians.' (Bible). We also went to visit Mary's House, where Mary was supposed to have been taken after the death of Jesus, her son. A priest, who lived nearby, got a lift from us to the bottom of the hill and was asked, 'Did Mary really live here?' The priest said, 'I don't know whether she lived here or not, but that doesn't matter. What matters, is that people of faith come together to remember Mary and the love of Jesus. It is such a peaceful place. As I was a librarian, the library at Ephesus meant a lot to me. I have a large poster of the library at Ephesus in my hallway at home.

'This library is one of the most beautiful structures in Ephesus. It was built in 117 A.D. It was a monumental tomb for Gaius Julius Celsus Polemaeanus, the governor of the province of Asia; from his son Galius Julius Aquila. The grave of Celsus was beneath the ground floor, across the entrance and there was a statue of Athena over it. Athena was the goddess of wisdom.

The scrolls of the manuscripts were kept in cupboards in niches on the walls. There were double walls behind the bookcases to prevent them from the extremes of temperature and humidity. The capacity of the library was more than 12,000 scrolls. It was the third richest library in ancient times after the Alexandria and Pergamum.

The facade of the library has two-stories, with Corinthian style columns on the ground floor and three entrances to the building. There are three window openings in the upper story. They used an optical trick that the columns at the sides of the facade are shorter than those at the centre, giving the illusion of the building being greater in size.

The statues in the niches of the columns today are the copies of the originals. The statues symbolize wisdom (Sophia), knowledge (Episteme), intelligence (Ennoia) and valor (Arete). These are the virtues of Celsus. The library was restored with the aid of the Austrian Archaeological Institute and the originals of the statues were taken to Ephesus Museum in Vienna in 1910.

There was an auditorium, which was for lectures or presentations between the library and the Marble Road, that was built during the reign of the Emperor Hadrian.'

(www.ephesus.us/ephesus/celsuslibrary.htm).

Libraries have always been very special places for me. I visited the local library on Longhill Estate from a very early age. I was so geared up to be a librarian, that I thought it was strange that I hadn't thought about this as a profession until the age of 26, when I fell into the profession what seemed to be by accident.

It was again lovely to find the link between Hull and Scotland, with the Carnegie Libraries. Andrew Carnegie was born in Dunfermline in 1835. So sad now to see the decline in libraries and government funding being taken away. It is an attack on the poor, yet again.

It was really special being in the presence of Bulent as we travelled around Turkey. Everyone seemed to know him and treated him with great respect. He had a very powerful aura around him and people seemed to bow when they saw him.

The first six months at Chisholme House have always stood out in my life like a beacon of light. I was given so many gifts, and 'sudden elegancies.' I was always surprised by the beauty of the place, even the pans in the kitchen and the plates we ate from and the way we laid the table in a particular way, so that its beauty shone through. I have always loved the Willow pattern plates that we eat from, and I have some at home so that it always reminds me of the beauty of life and helps me to remember with gratitude, His gift to me.

I didn't always find it easy at Chisholme, as much as I loved being there. I hadn't had much experience in a kitchen, for example, having come from a home that didn't have much food. My mam used to like the kitchen to herself, so I was never really shown how to cook. I can't remember that anyway. It proved really difficult, especially as cooking is an integral part of the course at Chisholme.

I used to get very anxious whenever I was told that I would be in the kitchen. I seemed to do everything wrong and was always shouted at. I thought at the time, that esoteric education meant I would be shouted at and that it was something I had to accept. But, I realise now, that it was not acceptable to be shouted at for not knowing what to do in the kitchen. If anything, I should have been shown what to do. I have missed a great learning opportunity on the first six month course and I now have a fear of the kitchen, and I am envious of anyone who can go in there and feel at home, and that is possibly everyone who has passed through the doors of Chisholme, except me.

When in the kitchen we used to have to read the Notice to Cooks before we started working in the kitchen.

'Now know this – that cooking is an art...

It is also an integral part of esoteric training because it is a two-fold means of service: service to humanity and service to the food prepared.

There is no higher state than that which a man can reach; all other forms of life in this world find their possibility of reaching a higher state through their conjunction with man. The only possibility for the sublimation of some minerals, vegetables and animals in a higher state of life is through cooking. That is why the sect which has aligned itself to the great saint Jalaluddin of Rum, the Mevlevi, refer to the esoteric education of the novices as cooking, and to achievement as taste.

Those who use ingredients of food without consideration of providing the best possible means of an ingredient's expression are devaluing service, awareness and value of life. Therefore, cooking is not a mixture of ingredients but a harmonious composition of artistic value, nutrient and transcendent, giving the possibility of the best expression to the ingredients as well as to the composition in general. It should be undertaken only in an attitude of deep respect and consideration and full awareness of the bounty and clemency in the Divine order.

Note - that there is no expression of divine manifestation devoid of beauty. Beauty of taste (dhawq) is an absolutely necessary ingredient of the essential (in all senses) composition. Had it been in the Divine order of things that mankind should graze, there would have been no need for cooking at all, but such not being the case, it is erroneous to think that all value in vegetables is only in a raw or under-cooked ingestion. Therefore certain fruits and vegetables have to be cooked properly before they can be eaten. The human being has neither tripe nor crop. Hence it is an incalculable error to think mankind could or should imitate avian or bestial mores.

Know then, that cooking is a responsibility in awareness wherein under-cooking or over-cooking are equally reprehensible and a clear oversight.

May the help (himma) of the great saint who was Rumi's personal cook till his death, Shamsuddin Ateshbaz Wali, be upon you who undertake to serve in this kitchen.'

(Bulent Rauf (1911–1987) founder of The Chisholme Institute).

Considering this is such an important part of the education, I feel that I was very short changed.

Fortunately, I can cook at home, enough to make meals for family and friends, which I very much enjoy. I feel closer to the saying of the nun Sister Agatha in her book A Nun's Story, where she writes:- Through all of life's experiences, cooking meals has been my way of getting to know people, serving them and loving them.'

When I had finished my first course in 1987, I went back to Chisholme periodically. I had always wanted to do the Second Course, but didn't have the resources. In 2010, I had the possibility of attending the second course, but I didn't know if I had the stamina to retreat from the world for six months. So I decided to take a week long course to see if I could be there for a week. If I couldn't be there for a week, I knew that I wouldn't last six months.

When I returned to Chisholme House on the 4th July 2010 for a week long course, I wrote the following whilst I was there, sitting in my bedroom.

The trees are talking in the bustling wind; the twilight sun flickering through the leaves. The smell of the beautiful wildflowers placed lovingly in a blue-patterned vase. The sun strengthening and fading with my every breath – the birds gently reminding me that they are still there.

I prayed to have been given a room in the house; and my prayers have been answered most generously. How fortunate am I? This is a world away from everything I have known; from all experiences, good or bad of the past; and just in the moment now, I feel renewed, energized. To love this moment, to see this moment, to feel this moment – is to love Him and to know His Love.

What do I fear before I enter this retreat, this world that is at Chisholme House? I am happy with my own company for in it I can think of Him. I can stay in retreat forever.

A proper little hermit; praying and wanting for nothing. Here, you face your reality.

Poem:
My burning Heart : The love Poems of Rumi

'My heart is burning with love
All can see this flame
My heart is pulsing with passion
Like waves on an ocean.

My friends have become strangers
And I'm surrounded by enemies
But I'm free as the wind
No longer hurt by those who reproach me.

I'm at home wherever I am
And in the room of loves
I can see with closed eyes
The beauty that dances.

Behind the veils
Intoxicated with love
I too dance the rhythm
Of this moving world.

I have lost my senses
In my world of loves.'

Yes, it was difficult for me to go down for the evening meal.
I'm a stranger, but no, I am not a stranger and never was: not
to the people who have certainty; I am neither friend, nor
stranger.
The meal was beautiful: soup and bread and fruit – a most
excellent meal.

I feel lost when all are rushing around; preparing the table – doing.

I become totally incompetent whilst I am here, helpless: from being someone who is independent and capable, I become childlike and incapable – I am afraid of this and do not understand why. Totally dependent.

Tonight, the person in charge of the course told us about the options we had for proceeding with the Fusus al Hikam, (written by Ibn Arabi in the 13th Century). We could read the Fusus for the whole week, or we could read bits of the Fusus and other pieces, depending on what came up for us during the day. The second one probably sounded the better option for me, as I have not really read the Fusus much before: I have attempted it: it is very difficult to read on your own; so I am hoping for a lot of insight into it.

I think we are looking at various chapters about the Names - Ayan al thabita.

In this room, there is absolute peace: The sound of the wind rustling through the trees can be heard; but inside this room there is perfect calm and stillness.

The most overwhelming love and compassion envelops me in this place.

Monday 5th July 2010

This time in 2004 I had experienced something bad. Yesterday in the year 2004, my mother had an accident. I had taken her on holiday to Scarborough and she fell down some steps whilst going to get her tea in the hotel. I should have been looking out for her and I had rushed off in front to get in the queue for food.

Mam really suffered – we went to the hospital where she was treated really badly – it was heartbreaking. It was the most horrendous time of my life. If I could have taken the pain from her and carried it myself, I would have.

She hadn't broken anything, but the pain was very bad. My brother came to collect us in the car and it was difficult for us to get her in because she was in so much pain.

At work they had no sympathy for me and it was the beginning of the end for my job. My manager treated me so badly; sending me to occupational health because I was crying about my mam's accident. (I showed too much emotion, apparently). Because I wanted a few days off to look after my mam they did not like it and it started off a spiral of illness and stress due to vindictive and unsupportive management.

I slept well last night. To be at ease on one's own is a very good thing: but for me it is too easy. My problem is getting out there and mixing and talking and being friendly. It's hard work, isn't it?

The readings this morning were amazing. With Avi in charge and making it so clear, I begin to understand what the difference is between hidden and apparent – Batin and Zahir. We looked at Wisdom and Wisdoms.

Having just come from the garden and weeding, I realised the connection between the word and what I was doing in the garden.

I was picking rocket leaves, I was in the little greenhouse that said, Danger, Keep Out. It was falling apart, but all sorts of vegetables and plants were still growing there.

The sun was brilliant white and a warm breeze passed through the shed, banging the tarpaulin that had been placed over the door.

As I was picking the rocket it reminded me of what I had just read that morning in Extracts from the Introduction to the Ottoman translation of and Commentary on the Fusus al-Hikam concerning the Names and Qualities.

'But when there has been manifestation of the Ipseity, [itselfness, for its own sake] the forms of the Qualities, which are the Realities of the Names, appear and differentiate themselves one from the other – as do the leaves and the fruit etc. The differentiation happens because of the Qualities inherent in the Names and this first happens in the presence which is the Presence of Knowledge of the Ipseity. For each Name there is a portion of manifestation which is delineated to that Name. Therefore, some of the leaves are covering and large – which are in front – some of the leaves are small and hidden, some of the leaves are small and obvious, some of the leaves are large and hidden, some of the leaves overlap and some do not overlap and are not overlapped.'

Of course, I didn't think all this whilst picking rocket leaves with the sweet, warm air moving magically around me in the brilliant sunshine. No, what I thought was how the rocket plants are rocket plants and yet each leaf is unique; and how silky smooth each leaf felt in my hand, and upon eating the rocket leaves at the evening meal, how extra specially tasty the rocket leaves were and how they connected with me and I them, physically, mentally, emotionally, virtually and intellectually.

Tuesday 6th July 2010

I worked in the garden yesterday.

Some of the leeks had weeds wrapped around them, and it was difficult to get them out – they still looked healthy though.

This bedroom that I am staying in is so peaceful and quiet. I love it so much. I will go and see Bulent soon. God willing. With help I will cook.

Nafs-i-rahman (the Compassionate Ipseity).

Compassionate Ipseity is an added ipseity to the Ipseity. I have imposed upon Myself nafs-i-Rahman.

Thursday 8th July 2010

Yesterday evening I went up the hill to see Bulent. Upon the hill – alone – you get the sense of magnitude that is His world.

What a beautiful place to have been buried: All are from God and to God they shall return.

I love being on my own because then I cannot do anything wrong.

At Chisholme I am afraid of doing wrong. Every time I feel like that I want to leave. I can't face it and at other times, when I am happy, there is no other place in the world that I would rather be.

Friday 9th July 2010

God leads to proper direction whom He wishes.

Wisdom and Wisdoms

Wisdom is never acquired but always received. When given to whom God may choose to give, and once given to whomsoever, 'great good is established.'

It was a very informative week and I gained a greater understanding and new insights of the study due to the knowledge of the supervisor and the quality of explanations and conversation of all the participants. I very much valued and appreciated the company of those, both on the course and members of staff and visitors.

The facilities of the school are outstanding. I was welcomed on arrival and I stayed in a beautiful, peaceful room and the food at all times was of a high standard.

It was because of this week I decided to take the second six month course at Chisholme starting October 2010.

12

Second Course October 2010 - March 2011

'In the midst of winter, I found there was within me an invincible summer.' (Albert Camus).

I went up to Chisholme to undertake the second course, two days before it was due to start, and stayed at a hotel in Carlisle before I entered Chisholme. This was an enormous step for me. I was leaving the world behind and going into retreat. So I spent the day before in Carlisle going into cafes, drinking coffee and eating cakes and sitting, just sitting, thinking and chatting to the local people. I was alone, but I knew, never alone. All the people in the past who had hurt me, were no longer part of my beautiful life. I was totally and utterly free. Freedom to live in peace is the most essential part of the human life; yet so many people want to destroy the peace of others, instead of concentrating on their own peace.

This time was the most amazing and magical time I had. The people on the course were from all over the world. I shared a room with a beautiful woman from Indonesia called Eva. There were ten people on my second course, including me, and the first course was running at the same time; so Chisholme was a pretty full place at the time. Very exciting.

For me being at Chisholme is living the life that should be led. I was in a magical world, far more magical than Hogwarts and I didn't need a wand to weave a lace of magic, surrounding me at every moment. A life that anyone can have, if they realise.

I'll give a few examples; it's all to do with trust.

The first story relates to my first course. I had gone back to Hull for Christmas, after my return from the Turkey trip. On travelling back to Hawick, I arrived there at about a quarter past eight on December 30th 1986. The street lights were on but, it was very dark, snowing, freezing. Nothing was open. What was I to do? I didn't have a mobile phone in those days. I went to the telephone box in the main street. I rang the number for Chisholme House to see if someone could give me a lift. I heard the phone being picked up on the other side but I couldn't hear anyone on the other side; but I continued to talk as if they could hear me. 'Hello, I don't know if you can hear me, but I can't hear you. I've just arrived in Hawick and I wonder if someone can come and get me. I'm standing outside the Green Café. Thank you.'

I repeated this a few times, and saying I couldn't hear them. I had to trust that they had heard me.

I waited outside the Green Café, and waited and waited. It took about twenty minutes and a car pulled up. I was so relieved. They had heard me. Thank God.

The second story is about an incident on the Second Course when I went home after the Turkey Trip to sort out my finances over the Christmas. Whilst we waited at the hotel in Turkey, the news was bad for travelling as everywhere was snowed in. The airports were completely shut down, and we didn't know what we were going to do; but at breakfast the next day, the leader of the group, Hakim, told us to be ready to travel. We got out of the airport with no trouble at all. We had arrived back at Edinburgh airport at about 10pm on the 20th December 2010. I was going to stay at the airport that night and then catch a bus the next morning to get a train to Hull. I sat on a seat and watched everyone depart for their coach. Something moved inside of me and I looked at the bus that went to Edinburgh and just got on it. It wasn't even a feeling that I was doing the right thing, it was 'letting go'.

I had very little money until I got back to Hull to transfer funds; so I really needed to stay at a fairly reasonable hotel and I knew that the hotels in the centre of Edinburgh would be expensive. As the bus travelled along Princes Street; I happened to look to my left and saw 'Easy Hotel' I got off at the next stop and walked back along the icy, dark street to the hotel.

The door of the hotel was firmly shut so I pushed the button on the intercom and the receptionist let me in. She said she thought that all the rooms were full or not made up, but she had a look and sure enough there was one room left at £24.00. I was so grateful. The room was the smallest room – no windows, just a bed that filled the whole room and a small toilet and shower. Amazing really and just outside my room there were vending machines where I could get coffee, crisps and chocolate. I got my drink and food and settled down for the night. I was safe.

I left at 6 am the next morning and went to MacDonalds for breakfast. Even that early in the morning there was a lot of movement of people and traffic in the centre of Edinburgh. I wasn't sure of what train I would catch. I was just trusting. It seemed that everywhere I went with my suitcase I had men wanting to carry it for me. Something that doesn't happen normally. A man carried my suitcase down the stairs. The train to Hull left at 7am. It was lovely and practically empty. However, the weather was still closing in with snow and fog. It was a difficult travel and the message came through that it was going no further and stopping at Newcastle.

It was chaos when we arrived at Newcastle train station. There were hundreds of people trying to find out what was going on and where they would get a train and even if there was one. I heard there was a train to Selby at a certain platform, but when I got to the platform, it changed again. I, along with others, ran from one platform to another carrying our heavy bags and suitcases. I was at the main entrance when I heard yet again, that the platform the train was coming on was across the other side. I had practically given up – it was sheer madness. Another angel came to my rescue. A man picked up my suitcase and said he would help me to the train. I followed and was so grateful. He was carrying my suitcase and his own bags.

The train pulled in just as we were all crowding onto the platform. It was clearly full and the man threw his and my suitcase onto the train, and I stood at the doorway until I reached Selby. I got off at Selby and looked at the monitor. There was a train in ten minutes to Hull and then after that the trains to Hull said, cancelled, cancelled, cancelled. I was about to catch the last train to Hull that day and it wasn't even 12 noon.

When I arrived back home and rang my brothers to let them know that I was back, they couldn't believe it. 'The whole of the world has stopped and no one is getting home, and you've travelled from Turkey. How?'

On the way back to Chisholme on the last day of the year the weather was even worse. I left my flat at 6am and could hardly walk on the snow and ice – it was snow upon snow, upon ice, and it was so difficult to move. I just got to the top of the driveway of the flats and saw the long street ahead to get me to the bus stop and I thought, 'I can't, I can't do it!' Just as I was about to turn back a complete stranger came out of a side street. A jolly man, and as I found out later, called Martin.

'Ah, are you going to the bus stop?'

'Yes,' I said, startled.

'Come on then,' he said, grabbing my suitcase.

He carried it all the way to the bus stop, and we arrived just as the bus showed up. I thanked him profusely.

The journey back to Chisholme was somewhat amazing. All the trains I needed to catch were on time and the journey was without any incident. Considering the bad weather, this was truly amazing, and I received help all the way along from gentlemen helping me with my suitcase. On the coach from Edinburgh to Hawick, the weather closed in around me. It was really quite spooky.

When I got back to Hawick, I got a taxi. I went and asked a young taxi driver if he could take me to the Chisholme Institute. He said yes. When I got to Chisholme; they asked, 'how on earth did you get a taxi because none of them are coming out here?' The journey was quite amazing; and how I got back without a hitch, is to me, a miracle.

So, back in the snow filled land that was Chisholme, I settled back into retreat life for the next three months.

The next story relates to signs and symbols that I feel are around us all the time, but sometimes we are just so busy to see them. Many happenings at Chisholme are very symbolic and point, I believe, towards a Higher Being.

One cold October morning at 6am, I was feeling 'trapped', I felt suddenly, that I needed to go for a walk and clear my head. I got ready and armed with a torch, I walked into the darkness to the main road. It was quite spooky. I turned my light off, because I didn't want to attract anything to me. As I was walking towards the main road, I could see, what I thought were lights, hovering in the sky. I gasped, because I thought, 'Oh no, I may be having a close encounter, and if I'm taken up with them, noone will know where I am.'

I heard a noise getting louder and louder and closer and closer to me. I then realised that I needed to turn my light on just in case it was a car coming up the long winding drive. On one side of me there was a large mound, that I couldn't climb up and on the other side of me a long drop. I was on a corner. Suddenly, I was faced with a Juggernaut that stopped at my feet, my nose inches away from it. I gulped as I looked into the cabin to where the man was sitting. He shook his head. I didn't know which way to move. At first I tried to climb the mound, but couldn't, so I had to find a place that dropped away on the other side, which I just managed. The Juggernaut went past me, and then another one, and another one, three in all. Had I not turned my torch on when I did, I believe I would have been knocked down.

When I told this story in conversation back at Chisholme, it turned out that the word juggernaut is derived from the Sanskrit Jagannatha (Devanagari) 'world-lord', combining jagat ('world') and natha('lord'), which is one of the names of Krishna found in the Sanskrit epics.

'The English loanword juggernaut in the sense of 'a huge wagon bearing an image of a Hindu god' is from the 17th century, inspired by the Jagannath Temple in Puri, Odisha (Orissa), which has the Ratha Yatra ('chariot procession'), an annual procession of chariots carrying the murtis (statues) of Jagannâth, Subhadra, and Balabhadra. Balabhadra, also known as Balarama or Baladev, is known to be one of Krishna's greatest worshippers, who was reincarnated as Krishna's elder brother.

The first European description of this festival is found in

the 14th-century The Travels of Sir John Mandeville, which apocryphally describes Hindus, as a religious sacrifice, casting themselves under the wheels of these huge chariots and being crushed to death. Others have suggested more prosaically that the deaths, if any, were accidental and caused by the press of the crowd and the general commotion.

The term is used in Charles Dickens' The Life and Adventures of Martin Chuzzlewit, published in 1844, to describe the love-lorn sentiments of Mr. Augustus Moddle, the 'youngest gentleman' at Mrs. Todgers': 'He often informed Mrs. Todgers that the sun had set upon him; that the billows had rolled over him; that the Car of Juggernaut had crushed him; and also that the deadly Upass tree of Java had blighted him.'

The figurative sense of the English word, with the idea of 'something that demands blind devotion or merciless sacrifice' became common in the mid-nineteenth century. For example, it was used to describe the out-of-control character Hyde in Robert Louis Stevenson's Dr. Jekyll and Mr. Hyde. Other notable writers to have used the word this way range from H.G. Wells and Longfellow to Joe Klein. Bill Wilson in Twelve Steps and Twelve Traditions of Alcoholics Anonymous describes 'self-sufficiency' in society at large as being a 'bone-crushing juggernaut whose final achievement is ruin.' To the contrary, Mark Twain (autobiography, vol 2), describes Juggernaut as the kindest of gods. Any pretensions to rank or caste do not exist within its temple.' (Wikipedia).

Looking back at my time at Chisholme, it was a time of great privilege and hope. It was the perfect time for me to be there. I met the most amazing people and I'm grateful that they are still in my life to this day. People from all over the world with very different lifestyles to mine; with different thoughts and politics, yet united with the One belief and the importance of the Dignity of Man.

One of my favourite things at Chisholme was helping with the ducks. Letting them out in the morning was far easier than getting them back into the pens at night. I could let them out and feed them by myself, but sometimes it took three of us to get them back into the pens at night. They were Muscovy Ducks and could be quite comical. There was one in particular that did not want to be put to bed at night and stood on the roof of the hutch, looking down at us. He seemed to have a Mohican hair style and he had a real attitude. Sometimes we could only get this duck in by catching him in mid-flight.

It was decided on the second half of the course that the students could have a Sunday off to do what they wanted. I went for long walks and took up painting again. I hadn't painted for years, and it was so wonderful to start painting again.

Me, walking in the snows in the grounds of Chisholme 2011

It was thanks to Shane, who had lived at Chisholme for many years, and was born in Hull also, that I started painting again. He gave me a box of new watercolour paints, a brush and some paper.

When I painted my first picture, which was the scene from my bedroom window at Chisholme, he was so enthusiastic with praise, that it encouraged me to do more. Sadly, Shane died recently, he was six months younger than me. He will be greatly missed at Chisholme, and it will be strange not to see him there when I visit again. He was a great artist and poet and I love his poetry, here is one from his book, 'My Heart is Too Big For My Pacemaker'.

The Heart

'The heart is the place
which perceives love

The divine inspiration
is given here

Look deeply into that
most intimate heart

It is the beginning
and end of all life

The origin of becoming
and the reason for all beauty

When time holds no sway
eternity enters in'

During my time on the second course, there was the blossoming romance between me and Allan. Actually, I didn't want a romance at Chisholme, because I wanted to concentrate on my course, and I had also seen too many romances there that ended badly. So we decided to play it cool and start seeing each other when we returned to our lives outside of Chisholme.

We met up in York to see each other at first and then, when we got to know each other better, he would stay with me in Hull and I would go and stay with him in Scotland. It was on one of his visits to York, when he got on his train to go back to Scotland, that I realised I didn't want to live without this man. I missed him every time he was away from me, so I was delighted that when I went to visit him for Christmas in 2011, he proposed to me at the Shrine of St Margaret of Dunfermline Abbey on my birthday. It seemed very appropriate, as St Margaret is the patron saint of wives and mothers. We married on St Margaret's day in November 2012.

So all the difficulties I had getting to Chisholme – what with giving everything up and not having a job to go back to; towards the end of the course I started to get worried as to what I would do for a job when I got back to Hull. I had to pay my mortgage and other bills after all.

When I got back to Hull I started job hunting with a vengeance. I signed on at the job centre and job agencies and sent off my cv to many other places.

I saw a job advertised for a call centre at the minimum wage and went for an interview.

Tricia and Allan taking a break outside Chisholme House
on our 6 month residential retreat

The young man who interviewed me told me to look around and see that it was all young people, and he thought that I might not fit in for that reason, being 51 years old. I smiled at him and left.

When I went to the jobcentre they asked me how I got on at the interview, so I told them. The next thing I knew was that I was called back to the call centre and shown to another room with older people; shown how to work the telephones and was told that I could start the following Monday. What a turn up for the books. At least I had something to go to so that I could at least pay my bills, even though I wasn't particularly happy about it.

I was sitting outside McCoys café enjoying a cup of coffee on the Friday afternoon, before I was to start work, when I received a telephone call from one of the agencies that I was registered with.

'How would you like to work at Beverley County Council, typing letters?' The voice on the other end of the 'phone asked. 'It starts on Monday.'

'Great, I'd love to. Do I have to be interviewed?'

'No, you have already been interviewed by us and we are putting you forward for the job, you just need to turn up on Monday.'

I was so relieved to hear this; I felt so much more comfortable typing in an office, rather than being on the telephone in a call centre. Nothing wrong with that, it's a decent job, but I wasn't used to it.

I loved working in Beverley, but it was only a temporary job. I was fortunate to meet someone I had worked with at the Jobcentre, and she told me of a job that had just become available in a place she had moved to at the Interchange in Hull. Someone had just left and they needed someone quickly. She told me to get my cv in quick, which is what I did.

I was interviewed and got the job of Reservations Clerk, where I stayed until I married in November 2012. I loved this job; although it was least money I had ever earned, I met some of the most amazing people, and I also found my cousins. It was great finding Emma and her mother, my cousin Elaine. Due to circumstances, we had never met, so it was great to be able to catch up, and we still meet up every time I'm in Hull.

There were many people who seemed to think this job was beneath me, (there are a lot of snobs out there), but let me tell you, it was a great job. It was right in the centre of town as well and the day was always so exciting. I have loved all my jobs and never seen any as being greater than the other. The only thing that was different was the pay. Strangely

enough, the more I earned, the less I seemed to do.
When I moved to Scotland, I worked at Fife Council in a business support role. I enjoyed this also, until I retired, due to ill health.

13

Life in Scotland

'That which strikes the oyster, does not damage the pearl.'
(Rumi).

It is difficult starting up in a new place at any age, but especially when you are in your later years. Being 52 years old when I moved to Scotland, I found it particularly difficult to start afresh, find a job and make new friends.

I loved the anonymity at first – I didn't know anyone and they didn't know me. It was great. I concentrated in the first few months on getting a job, which was proving very difficult. I managed to get the interviews, but it was very hard securing a job, and I needed one to pay my bills.

I'd say, it took me about 2 full years before I settled down in Kirkcaldy. I got a job at Fife Council and made new friends. I can walk down the street in Kirkcaldy now and say hello to at least five people I know. I'm quite proud of that. And also, I'm so pleased with the friends I have made and the beautiful people who have made my life so happy here in Scotland.

My world is as optimistic as it has always been. Maybe the power of positive thinking. Don't get me wrong. The world is in a mess, but then it's always been in a mess. However, I come across heroes every day of my life. Ordinary people who do extraordinary things and the world never hears about it, but these are the people who keep the world spinning. The man I see outside my window who picks up litter at 7am every morning near the shops. People who say good morning and smile. People who don't have a hidden agenda, and would go out of their way to help you. People who see the good in everyone, even, seemingly, lost causes. Over the past few years I have lived through a Scottish Referendum and an EU Referendum with the call for another Scottish Referendum, and more recently a call for another EU referendum. These are not easy days. There seems to be a lot of bitterness and divide in certain quarters; but all-in-all, the ordinary people want to unite and be inclusive and live in peace.

I have friends from all over the world and I see what their lives are like instantly by Facebook and Skype and I can keep in touch with family in the same way. In a world where everything seems so intimate and closer together, it is interesting that it looks further away and more separate than ever. Why is that? I wonder.

I can't believe some of the things that are happening in our society. How did we get to this?

I'm writing this during the year 2016 and have returned to Hull on a number of occasions throughout the year. I must admit I am a bit disappointed in the whole process of what is happening to prepare for the City of Culture 2017. I wanted to go to Hull to enjoy a coffee outside my favourite coffee house, but because of all the orange barriers around the city because of the roads having been dug up, it is very difficult to enjoy Hull. The art gallery is closed for a full year, until it is refurbished.

Some of the events for 2017 have been announced, and ordinary, working people are finding that they are priced way out of what they can afford. It is said that there are going to be a lot of free events. Already they have taken on hundreds of volunteers to help with events. I think it would have been lovely if people had been paid for these jobs; after all the money that is supposed to come in for 2017. I hope there is going to be a huge party for all the volunteers at the end of the year.

I saw that they were looking for the 'Face of Hull' for 2017 and were holding auditions. I thought a friend of mine would be ideal for the job; but when I saw the process of auditioning, it was horrid. They were using 4 red buzzers like they do on Britain's Got Talent and the X Factor. People were going to audition, because they had a dream of being a part of 2017 for a City they love. Why should they be buzzed off? All the candidates only had one minute; surely you should give people their dignity.

I wanted to be in Hull for the start of 2017, but that was not to be. On the 17th November 2016, the day after my 4th wedding anniversary, I was told by a surgeon at the Victoria Hospital in Kirkcaldy, that I had cancer. It was a rare cancer of the bile duct and if I could have an operation, it was a major operation and not an easy thing to undertake.

When you are told you have got cancer, your whole world changes in an instant. It is such a shock and I felt like it was the end, just like that. To hear that there was an operation which was major and I may not be able to have it, was devastating. Allan and I went to the chapel, held hands and cried and prayed.

If I could have the operation, I would have to go to Edinburgh Royal Infirmary to get it done as they were one of the few hospitals who specialised in this operation. The operation is called Whipple Surgery, named after the surgeon that devised it, Allen Oldfather Whipple.

I was told in the January of 2017, that I could have the operation and that I needed to build up my stamina before I went in for it, as the operation was so bad and it could take up to a year to recover from it, with all sorts of other problems arising. The outcomes, didn't look that great, but I didn't have any option. I was just grateful that I could get the operation. But even then, there were all sorts of risks associated with it.

For months before I was diagnosed, I was losing weight very slowly, and not realising. When I went out to cafes, I didn't fancy anything to eat. I didn't realise anything was wrong, but looking back, I suppose I should have done.

All through the months of September, and October 2016, I started to get sick every night. Every night I would come home from work and eat my tea and then lay on the settee, feeling awful. I knew that if I moved I would be sick, so I lay there all evening until bedtime, and then I had to move.

As soon as I stood up I would rush to the toilet and be sick, but I knew it wasn't the usual type of sickness, it seemed to be coming from a different place and I could see it was bile. For months, I didn't do anything about it, thinking it would pass and all would be well, but then I started to turn yellow and after an emergency scan was admitted to Victoria Hospital straight away.

The scan revealed that there was a blockage in the bile duct and I had to have a stent put in to clear the pathway. I also had a biopsy to see what the blockage was. They tried to reassure me that it was only a gallstone that had got stuck and they could just whip it out, but unfortunately, it wasn't as simple as that.

When I went to see the surgeon in Edinburgh, he told me of all the problems relating to having bile duct cancer and it was terrifying. I would never be the same again.

I was told to build up my stamina before I went in for the operation, so I walked into town every day. The weather was beautiful for the beginning of January/February 2017, and anyone looking at me walking light footed through the streets of Kirkcaldy, would think that I didn't have a care in the world. Despite the stent, I felt to be at the fittest I had ever been and yet, I had a death sentence hanging over me. Waiting for the operation, I also became sick again, I was told that the stent may have to be replaced. I went to Hull in December 2016, not daring to think that it may be my last Christmas. On the day I was due to return to Kirkcaldy, I was too ill to travel.

'But she looked so well,' everyone kept saying. But that is what happened. One day I would be well and the next day I would be ill, shivering with flu like symptoms and feeling very sick. The hospital told me to get myself to a hospital if my temperature reached 39 degrees. It was just short of it every time, so I reached the date of my operation without having to have the stent removed and replaced.

I got my operation for bile duct cancer on February 27th 2017. My operation lasted six hours. They took out the cancerous bile duct, my gallbladder, part of my stomach, the head of the pancreas and I was told that the surgeon had to take out my liver and turn it upsidedown to get good veins, (or something like that; I was pretty much out of it when he gave me this news). All the bits that were left, were reattached to the bowel. I felt dreadful, yet when I was in the High Dependency unit, eating breakfast the next day, I felt quite contented. That was all about to change.

A man had been put into the next bed to me, and for some strange reason, he thought I was getting more attention than him and made a fuss about it, throwing his food around and even threatening me, calling me all sorts of names, which I won't repeat here. I never even saw the face of this person (I didn't want to), but they put me up to the main ward pretty quickly when he started to threaten me.

Before I went up to the ward, a female doctor had been brought in to calm the man down, after he had thrown his lunch tray onto the floor. The curtains went around him, and I could hear the doctor telling the man all about me and my operation, and the reason I was getting more attention, was that 'she could die at any moment.' She then proceeded to tell him about my operation. I laid in my bed horrified. I knew the operation was bad and that people had died on the operating table, but to actually hear it being spoken about to a complete stranger was such a shock.

I looked at the nurses who were at the foot of my bed, who were also in shock about what they were hearing. The man said he didn't care if I died, no one would care if he died. He said that I was crying and screaming all night and calling for God. This was simply not true. The nurses looked at each other and said 'he's lying.' The only time I spoke about God, was when a nurse came up to me at 3am in the morning when I had opened my eyes and said, 'Hello, we were getting worried about you.' I put my hand on her face and said, 'I thank God for you.' Then went back to sleep. The man in the next bed had obviously taken much offence at that. (I knew it was 3am as there was a large clock on the wall opposite).

With all the commotion with the man in the next bed; my heart rate started to go up. It was so fast I felt that it was coming out of my chest. The next thing I knew was that I was being whisked to a ward, to get me away from the man; he shouting verbal abuse after me. I felt so vulnerable and my heart going so fast, my thought was, 'Oh, I got through the operation, now I'm going to die of fright.' I didn't think to tell the nurses, I was so much in pain and I could hardly talk due to being so dry from the tube that had been down my throat for six hours.

During the evening, with hallucinations and distressed patients, I felt as if I was going to die. I seemed to go into another world and it was as if I was on some sort of roller coaster with a car made for two. There was a man beside me, although I didn't see him, it was more of a presence. I was looking down on what seemed to be gods and goddesses of India. I said to the person next to me, 'This is so beautiful'. I was looking down from above on the scene. The next thing I knew was that I was being shouted at by the nurses who seemed to have difficulty getting me awake. I awoke with a start at two nurses with terrified faces. They wanted to give me pain relief.

I woke up the next day, surprised that I was still there. I was told by one of the nurses to get myself into the shower. I could hardly walk and yet I wasn't given any help. I was terrified of falling, but I somehow managed to get myself into the shower. I slowly took all my clothes off, not caring what I looked like. I could hardly breathe because my mouth was so dry and I felt so, so ill.

I sat on the chair and switched on the shower with a great deal of difficulty. I allowed the water just to pour over me, there was nothing else I could do. I felt afraid and completely helpless. The water was everywhere and I couldn't clear it up, because I couldn't bend. I sat on the toilet seat to pull on my pyjamas and then went to the door.

I called over a nurse. I'm sorry, I've left a bit of a mess. I can't bend to clear it up. As I turned to walk to the bed, I heard one of the nurses say, 'I bet she's never cleaned a bathroom in her life.' I couldn't believe what I had just heard. They knew nothing about me, and they could say that to someone who had just had major surgery. How could they?

There was a female doctor at the foot of my bed. I said to her very quietly, because I could hardly speak, that I didn't think it was right that a doctor could give my details to another patient to try and keep him quiet, referring to the incident of the man in the next bed, the previous day. As I was telling her, I went to lay on my bed. I was exhausted.

The next thing, the doctor was yelling in my face. 'Doctors know not to give personal information, they wouldn't do a thing like that. You've got it wrong.' Her face nose to nose with mine.

I realised just how vulnerable I was, so I kept my mouth shut and continued to do so. I didn't feel safe at all in that hospital.

A bit later on I sat on a chair with my head on the table. Another, younger doctor came up to me and asked me if I was alright. I couldn't answer, my head flopping down. She put her two fingers on my neck and said something to a colleague. I went back down to the High Dependency Unit where they monitored my heart. I was sent for a scan on the Saturday evening and that night my surgeon came to me to say that there was an infection and they would have to operate again, although one half of the team didn't want to operate and the other half did. He asked me what I wanted. I said, 'I don't want another operation.'

The next day they decided to operate, so I had another four hour operation at 2pm on the Sunday. I was devastated. It knocked me for six. They had to give me another blood transfusion and I was on two lots of antibiotics as it was sepsis and the surgeon told me it was good they had operated, as it was my only chance of survival. I was taken back to the main ward again after a couple of days, much to my bewilderment. I found the ward quite difficult to take. Everything went into a blur and I could feel my body either fighting or just giving in. It was whilst they were giving me a blood transfusion that I slipped into another world yet again, only this time it was not as beautiful as the last one.

There was a beautiful island and I was standing on it; trees and birds and beauty. There was a male presence there like last time. He said, 'You see this as beautiful, don't you, but it isn't. It is pure evil.' And I could sense that through the beauty there was all sorts going on, death everywhere, with killings and hatred. It was awful and yet so familiar.

On the morning before my operation, the doctor who had shouted in my face came up to me and said with a smile on her face, 'you were very confused yesterday.' I didn't answer her, because I knew I wasn't confused. She said again, 'you were very confused yesterday.' I just looked at her and didn't answer, so she just walked away. I knew that if I was going to survive in that hospital it was best to 'play dead.'

Having now had my operation, which was very bad, me and Allan will be coming back to Hull to stay in the hotel we got married in, on our 5th wedding anniversary. I had a tough time after the operation. This book had to be put on hold, so I didn't get it to the printers by the start of the year of the City of Culture 2017 as I had intended.

After the operation, I laid on a bed settee for eleven weeks, not able to move or walk very well and it took a good four months to recover to the point where I could walk and go back to work and put the finishing touches to this book. My husband was marvellous throughout my illness and I thank him very much for all his love and support. The following is what I wrote for the pancreatic website to try and help people who were going through the same thing.

'I had Whipple surgery on Monday 27th February. There is no sugar-coating this; it was absolutely horrendous. I had a terrible time in the three weeks that I was in hospital and eleven weeks after. I had to have another operation within a week of the first one because I had contracted sepsis. This knocked me for six and I had terrible halucinations on the pain killers. I had two draining tubes and a feeding tube coming out of my stomach, pancreas area and gall bladder area. The pain from the entrances of these was terrible and the painkillers didn't seem to touch the pain.

When I came home from hospital after 3 weeks, I laid downstairs on the bed settee as I couldn't walk up the stairs and I could hardly walk at all. I could do nothing but lie on the bed settee and watch the television, but mostly I slept all day and all night, which was perhaps a good thing. Because of what happened to me, I went into a depression and sometimes all me and my husband could do was hold hands and cry. Crying was also difficult for me because my tear ducts had dried up as had my mouth. My mouth was very dry and painful. It took a good 15 weeks for my mouth to come back to normal. I drank lots of iced water and sucked on water melon and apples.

I couldn't eat very well and sometimes I was sick, but eventually, I could eat normally. Now and again if I overdo the eating I get sick, but otherwise, I'm fine.

I feel very much that I have been left to get on with it. I had a visit to the surgeon who operated on me at the end of April, and had the tubes and feeder taken out. I had lost 2 stone in the hospital, but managed to maintain my weight. The surgeon said he didn't want to see me again.

The oncologist also wanted to see me to go through chemotherapy options, but it was not for me, so I didn't go ahead with chemotherapy.

When I was very ill and depressed, I said to my husband, that had I known it was so bad, I wouldn't have gone through with it. However, today, 24th June 2017, I'm in a place where I can walk very well, eat very well and feel almost back to normal. I'm not taking any tablets. The only way I know I have had the operation is the scar and the areas I had the tubes in, which have healed really nicely. Also, the stomach area is numb and probably will be for some time, but I don't really notice that as I'm going about daily life. I'm returning to work in the first week of July.

What really got me through this was my marvellous husband, family and friends; all very supportive. As I was on the bed settee not being able to do anything, a lovely friend, who was only nineteen and who I used to work with, sent me an adult colouring book through the post with a set of coloured pens. I was so touched and just started to colour in, it meant so much to me as suddenly, I became interested again. I started to look at colour and fashion. I needed more clothes as I had lost so much weight.

Soon, I was up and walking better each day, even going into the town by myself and buying some new clothes.

I'm not sure what the future will hold, and I have read all the statistics and what people go through, and it is different for each person; but I'm taking each day as it comes and try to remain positive and do something each day.

It has been a really difficult time, but I feel that there is hope and I'm thankful to the surgeons and staff in both of my operations who saved my life.'

The Whipple Surgery is named after the Surgeon who performed this operation….. Allen Oldfather Whipple. I know this sounds strange, because my life was saved, but

I really wanted to hate this guy. After the operation I had felt totally brutalised and left for dead. It felt as if my whole body had been invaded and I felt so dreadful. So dreadful, that I can't really describe how awful it felt.

I found a book about Whipple's life and it helped me so much to understand the man, and even though he was a great surgeon, there were many similarities to our lives. I grew to love Allen Whipple, who had many tragedies in his own life, and I learned to be grateful, to him and the surgeons and teams who saved my life.

Looking back on this time, I realise what a special and precious time this was. Fighting for your life and praying and being closer to God and death, is quite something. There are no words to describe this happening, but facing your own and inevitable death, is very grounding, strangely enough.

My husband travelled to the hospital every day to see me. He was exhausted, but he continued to come and see me even though I told him not to. I couldn't make much conversation when Allan came to see me, but he would sit and hold my hand and read things to me.

I remember one piece in particular that I was particularly moved by:

'God speaks to each of us as he makes us,
then walks with us silently out of the night.

These are the words we dimly hear:

You, sent out beyond your recall,
go to the limits of your longing.
Embody me.

Flare up like a flame
and make big shadows I can move in.

Let everything happen to you: beauty and terror.
Just keep going. No feeling is final.
Don't let yourself lose me.

Nearby is the country they call life.
You will know it by its seriousness.

Give me your hand.'

Rainer Maria Rilke
Book of Hours, I 59
translation by Joanna Macy and Anita Barrows
Allan also read it in its original German, and it was very
beautiful. I felt his words wash over me in a healing way.

14

Sitting in Peace

'There's only one thing you need…and that one thing will not be taken away.' (The Bible, Luke 10:42).

I use the above quote from the Bible to emphasise the beauty of sitting in peace, being at peace with yourself and just doing nothing, but listening, observing, enjoying the moment as Jesus said to Martha about Mary. Martha was busy doing all sorts and she wouldn't sit down and rest, but Mary sat and listened to Jesus and just lived in the moment. Martha was angry and asked Jesus to tell Mary to help her in the kitchen. Jesus answered: 'Martha, Martha, thou art careful and troubled about many things, but there is only one thing you need and Mary hath chosen that good part, and that one thing will not be taken away from her.' This links to Psalm 27:4 which states: 'One thing have I desired of the Lord, that will I seek after; that I may dwell in the house of the Lord all the days of my life, to behold the beauty of the Lord and see Him in His temple.'

Since I left work completely in February 2018 due to the daily difficulties of having Whipple Surgery, I have involved myself in many different activities, all of which I have wanted to do in the past, but work has prevented me enjoying fully, as I didn't have the time or the energy to do it whilst I was working. Now I have a lot of time and I'm in the fortunate position to be able to do things that I've always wanted to do, and I can sit and rest anytime I want to without feeling guilty about it.

When I first came up to Scotland I was very busy trying

to find a job. It was very difficult and at first I was offered temporary jobs with agencies. What follows is a passage for my blog that I wrote some time ago, when I first came up to Scotland. The blog helped me to get through things and put them in perspective.

'It will be lovely to become a human again after being an automaton for the past few years. Places of employment just don't get it do they? We are humans, not machines. The less time you give us for 'performing' tasks, the more stress on the mind and body; the more illness, the more people being off sick. I'm a hard worker, I always have been, but the productivity levels now placed on the workers is totally unrealistic. Oh sorry, I forgot my place, as a temporary worker I have no rights and it doesn't matter if we get ill, you can just replace us.

I felt dreadful leaving work last night and I feel that there is a connection between our employment and the way society behaves. I came out of work angry and stressed.

It was only the hour-long journey back home that helped me calm down with the beautiful scenery that is the Fife Coastal Path.

Man is The Green Resource to be treasured and honoured for who and what we are, not dehumanised and demoralised. It can be done; and next week I shall take my breaks as usual, I shall go to the toilet when I need to and not hold on because I won't reach my target for the day. Stuff the targets, I do more than a days work.'

I love this poem written by my niece Nikki.

From Go Green Book 1992 written by young writers. The first one in the book is untitled by Nichola Jayne Turner (15)

'The very air we breathe,

is no longer fresh and sweet,
old beer cans and rubbish
litter in the street.

We are all to blame
for the problems that we face.
The destruction of our world,
is man's own disgrace.

But now the experts have
made us aware.
We must stop using aerosols,
polluting the air.
We must stop slaughtering animals
just for their fur.
We must put right our mistakes
and show that we care.

The time has come to
pay heed to the warning.
To begin afresh,
like a new day dawning.
Because now we know
that all those things are linked.
It's not just the animals
that might become extinct!'

'When there are no wind and waves in your mind, then wherever you are is all green mountains and trees. When there is evolutionary development in your nature, then everywhere you go you see fish leap and birds fly.' (Reflections on the Tao by Huanchu Daoren).

'On the life-work balance issue, I'm finding my new job difficult to get back from. However, I have come to the conclusion that I need to relax and enjoy the journey. Now that the nights are coming in lighter I can see the views across bay. Coming into Kirkcaldy over the hill is just breathtaking. How fortunate to see that every day. And when I get home, my lovely husband has cooked a fantastic, comforting meal. Weekend now, and it's my turn to look after him.'

Recently, I've been told that I may have post-traumatic stress disorder from the operation, and I have been in touch with the Maggie's Centre in Fife to ask for help. I am now taking a 10-week expressive art class and it is just amazing. I can't believe the help that it is giving me. I feel that it is a gift that is allowing me to express that which is hidden and buried within. I don't always understand why I am painting what I paint, but I know that it is coming from the heart. For example, I went to the class and I never know what I am going to create that day. I sit for a while and then get my materials. The person leading the class has all sorts of materials around the room that we can help ourselves to. On one particular day, I suddenly decided that I was just going to draw around my hands. As I did so, I noticed that by putting the two hands together on the page, it had created a heart shape in the middle. I adorned the hands with placing different coloured beads on the fingers and wrists, then coloured with a gold paint to make it look as if there were rings on the fingers. I also placed a yin yang symbol on the left palm and a fish with love written on it on the right palm. Then, I have no idea why, I made the nails into evil eyes. (I've never really understood 'the evil eye').

I thought that I had painted the hands because I have a trigger thumb which is painful, and I wanted to decorate the fingers to show that you can get through the pain with love, and I feel that I used the evil eye to ward off the pain, but that evening, when I was watching television, I saw an advertisement for a programme that would be on the following week about surgeons, and there on the full screen were the hands of a surgeon, just like the ones I had painted. And then I realised why I may have drawn the hands.

I was struggling with the aftermath of the operation, in that, I was incredibly grateful for the surgeons for saving my life, but I felt 'left for dead'. I felt so awful, that I couldn't bring together these two dichotomies, and suddenly, like a revelation, I saw that my life had been saved, and I wasn't left for dead, I just felt as if I were left for dead, and that is the big difference. I felt, that through the creative art, my heart, or inner knowledge was helping me see this revelation. It has helped so much for my road to recovery. I now believe that the hands I had drawn were actually the surgeons hands, and I was adorning them with love, because he had saved my life, and I put on the evil eyes as protection from the pain.

The final painting I did, on the last day of the art therapy class, was called, 'The Peacock and the Pearl.' I painted this to be positive. The peacock represented, the beauty of humans, and the song 'True Colours' and the pearl was from Rumi's poem, when he says '..that which strikes the oyster, does not damage the pearl.' It was a reminder to me, that the very essence of who I am, cannot be destroyed, no matter what I go through in life.

I feel that expressive art should be allowed in all schools as I think it would help the psyche in children and help them to express themselves when they sometimes feel lost. These sessions are not taught, it comes from within, whatever you feel is necessary to heal. A remarkable and fascinating process.

On 21st March, 2019, I had two pieces of my artwork exhibited in the F.E.E.L.S.19 exhibition in Edinburgh. 'Forget everything else, let's show,' is the brainchild of Linghong Wang, an Edinburgh University student, who had the vision one night to create a space where 'emotions come alive…a social project that provides a creative space to celebrate emotions.'

'At F.E.E.L.S., we collaborate with professionals to conduct emotion and art-related workshops and talks at the University of Edinburgh, to raise awareness of emotional well-being. Our aims are to break the stigma surrounding emotional expression and mental health and to motivate and inspire individuals to use creative arts to maintain good mental health.' (Publicity leaflet).

I went to help out on the first day of the two day exhibition. I thoroughly enjoyed it, and set up the art table and helped out on the registration desk. I was also asked to say a piece to camera about one of my art pieces.

Linghong, along with the team, did a magnificent job with this exhibition, and I hope it continues to bear fruit, as there seems to be a real need for it.

I met some amazing people that day, and I know it brought so much joy to a lot of people.

The Peacock and the Pearl

The Surgeon's Hands

15

Back To The Garden

'We are stardust, we are golden. And we've got to get ourselves back to the garden.' (Joni Mitchell).

Now that I have retired totally, I spend so much more time in the garden. Our garden is very overgrown with lots of trees. When I was working it was very difficult to keep it under control as we just didn't have the time or the energy. Now that I am retired, the garden is my joy.
The following is also taken from my blog before I became ill. 'My little seeds are growing nicely on the windowsill. It is so exciting to see them growing from the tiniest little seed. The miracle of life. I feel like a child again. I remember growing cress at school, but I didn't really 'feel' it as I do now.
The Soil Association have sent me my Phacelia seeds to 'Keep Britain Buzzing' (http://www.soilassociation.org/).
The other thing I'm trying to do whilst I grow my seeds is lose weight; especially with obesity being in the news all the time. There was a 'phone in on the radio the other day and large people were really getting a slating. There was one lone woman rang in and said that she could not believe what she was hearing and found it criminal that people could talk about larger people in that way and that it was cruel. I felt tears coming to my eyes as this was the one woman who spoke from the heart. How did we get to this, that we demonise people for being large?
I'm not saying there isn't a problem regarding obesity in society. It seems to be out of control and I do think it's linked with our separation from our natural environment

and the need to eat home grown foods. Also, working in the garden, working on the land, is a natural exercise.

I'm not making excuses, but my weight problem developed when I developed BPPV that started in 2000. My balance was affected and I gave up doing the exercises that I did every day in order to keep fit as any head movement sent me spinning and feeling sick.

There are exercises that you can do slowly to help with balance control.

My husband has been very good in helping to motivate me to lose weight. He has come up with ABLE, Agile, Balance, Lithe, Energetic. This all fits in with my lifestyle and the need to improve my health. My husband gives me inspiration.

Yesterday I was supposed to go to a beginner's gardening class. I didn't make it due to the weather. I will get there one day. Instead I looked around for seed boxes. Alison, at work, told me of the type of boxes that may be useful.

I've been looking at inspirational gardening and gardeners. Thanks to Wendy on facebook I saw this inspirational talk by Ron Finley. We do need to get back to the garden, as I suggested in one of my previous posts. (Ted talk online).

I'm not a natural gardener, I have to be honest; but I'm going to try harder.

I got married last November in Hull and moved into my husband's home in Kirkcaldy, Scotland. Allan's garden, our garden, is very full of various plants. I was saying to Allan yesterday that we need to see where we will plant things. I said, 'I'd love to grow strawberries.'

'We have strawberries,' he said. 'Where?' I asked.

'All over the garden,' he replied.

'How come?'

'I don't know, they were just there.'

I think the first thing I should do is take an inventory of what is in the garden.

In the meantime I am collecting lots of gardening tips from papers, magazines and gardening books.

I went to an excellent talk last night by Stephen Hirtenstein Human Being/Being Human: Awareness, ascension and the attaining of true happiness.

I thought afterwards about what it means to be human and how we treat each other and our environment. I thought about Apollo 13. I always know how it ends, but I could watch it again and again. I was there when it happened, i.e. I was one of the many glued to the television watching the drama unfold. I was only 10 years old, so I didn't realise how bad it was, but I can still sense the feeling of the household and how everyone was talking about praying for the safe return of the astronauts. In Le Monde paper it read. 'The whole human race is participating with them in the agony of their return.'

I saw a video this morning posted on Facebook and it was so beautiful, looking back at our earth from space and seeing its total beauty.

We've got to get ourselves back to the garden.

Just wondering about what I do at the moment to help to make the planet greener.

- I recycle paper, clothes, etc

- I travel on public transport

- Reduce, reuse, repair, recycle

- Buy local foods

- Grow my own - eventually

- Buy Fairtrade products where available

- Eat organic foods when I can

- Celebrate the beauty of life

- Turn off lights that are not necessary

There was a man who used to speak on Radio Humberside called Ernie Teal. He died at the age of 92. He was a real character who could tell you everything about the birds, bees, trees, gardening. He was a man of great wisdom and I learned a lot from him with the radio programme and his column in the Hull Daily Mail.

Many years ago I was a passenger in a car and a sparrowhawk killed a sparrow right in front of the window. It was a shock to see it. 'So much for God looking after the birds of the air,' I thought. This also came as a vision to me when I was in hospital and it seemed to be horrendous, but it is all part of ecology. Ernie puts it like this in one of his poems, 'The Breeze.'

'Gently the breeze plays with the blossom of the cherry trees,
spilling the petals and disturbing the bees,
caressing the beeches and rippling the corn,
carrying messages of another dawn.

A blackbird awakening fluted his song!
But alas his greeting was not for long!
A sparrowhawk up aloft that morn and
keen to feed her newly born,
clutched the chorister from his bower.

To the songster had come at this early hour,
a death as swift as that hawk in flight:
more would die 'ere day turned night.
For nature is ever red in tooth and claw.
He who made all things decreed it so.

The feathers of the innocent fluttered down,
covering the earth in a chastening gown.
That gentle breeze played with them
as it passed by
with a whisper, or was it a sigh.'

Where I used to live at my flat in Hull, my bedroom backed onto the beautiful shared garden, with a massive cherry tree, plum trees and trees all in the neighbouring gardens. The dawn chorus was music for the heart. My heart leapt for joy every time I heard it.
The gardens and grounds were looked after by outside companies that the flat committee paid, so I didn't have anything to do with the garden. Now that I have a garden, here in Scotland, things are going to be different.
In my new garden I am going to plant herbs and flowers and vegetables and I'm going to have a meditational labyrinth.
My friend Karina bought me some cornflower seeds for my birthday. I'm going to start with those.
I put water out in the garden for the birds, as it has been an incredibly hot summer, without rain. I have such great pleasure in watching the birds flap their wings in delight as the water splashes over them. They enjoy it so much and I feel great joy after watching them.'
Recently, I took a cookery course in Kirkcaldy, and I'm surprised at how much I loved it. I have always been afraid

of the kitchen, as I have mentioned in other chapters, but I did want to gain confidence, and even though I'm much older, I learned a great deal. I can now go into the kitchen anytime and make soups and meals and bake. I came to the realisation in this new found love of food, that food really is connected with our whole being and how we are. If we eat well, we maintain our proper weight.

I realised also, that it is just as easy making vegetable soup, for example, as it is opening a tin of soup and heating it up, but at least you know what is going into your soup. There is also such enjoyment in cooking. The next step for me is growing a lot more fruit and vegetables. There is nothing more rewarding than eating the food you have grown.

It was for the first time on December 25th 2018, that I cooked my first Christmas meal at the age of 59. Is that appalling, or not? My husband couldn't believe that I hadn't cooked a Christmas meal before, but as I explained to him, first my mam cooked for me, and friends, and I'd also go to restaurants, and then, my beloved husband cooked my Christmas meals for me. It just goes to show that you are never too old to learn new skills.

My eyes have been opened since my 'near death experiences'. I do see things differently. I've just started buying monkey nuts and I cannot believe I haven't seen the beauty in them before. They are an incredible thing, and all for us; how much more is a human being so beautiful. As Shams Tabrizi, spiritual instructor of Rumi, said, 'The whole universe is contained within a single human being - you. Everything that you see around, including the things that you might not be fond of and even the people you despise or abhor, is present within you in varying degrees.' If we were really aware of this, how much more would we respect each other and be kinder to each other.

Afterword

'We should be careful of each other, we should be kind, while there is still time.' (Philip Larkin, The Mower).

Remembering the young girl sitting in the classroom and looking out at the hedgehog and wishing she were free; the teenager playing truant and wishing she were free; the girl at work longing for the holidays and wishing she were free, I see a very privileged and carefree life.

And now, as I am older and have faced death, how I long for those days where I belonged and was living a happy and carefree life.

I know a lot of people who have said, 'Regrets, I don't have any. Life is too short for regrets.' I say, 'Regrets, I have plenty; things I have said, that I shouldn't have said; things I have done, that I shouldn't have done and hurt other people and myself; a cruel word, a silly action. Will feeling remorse be enough to grant me pardon?

I look back now, at the age of 59, life went by seemingly with the blink of an eye. How I wish to be that little girl again, looking out of the window at the hedgehog, her whole life in front of her. I was on the train recently from Hull to Kirkcaldy and I saw a group of school children at their sports day, full of life and excitement and I was transported back to my younger years. It reminded me of Tom Hanks in Big, when he is trying to decide if he should stay as an adult or go back to his younger self. He visits his school and sees all the things he would miss if he didn't go back.

When I feel that longing to return to my younger days, I'm reminded of Ecclesiastes 3 'To every thing there is a season, and a time to every purpose under the heaven.' I have had my days in the sun.

And from another tribute to 'The Last Hedgehog,' Pam Ayres writes:

'Like the owl which hunts the mouse
Like swifts returning to a house
We fit like interlocking rings
Neatly in the scheme of things.
This is the truth, these are the facts,
The whole of nature interacts.'

Since I was diagnosed with cancer and had my Whipple operation to try and cure it, I have seen life differently. Life has become more colourful; more wonderful. I took life for granted. It has gone by in a flash. I'm still here, but I'm aware that time is not on my side. I'm trying to make the most of the time I have. Throughout my book, I see the connections, the 'sudden elegancies', the golden thread, that runs throughout my life; life itself has communicated with me and I have not always been aware of it. It is the Law of Three in action; all the things that seem to be a happy coincidence is life itself communicating with us, letting us know it is on our side. It is with us. It connects every single one of us.

What got me through my terrible ordeal was the love and support of people near me and from all over the world, praying for me and offering support. Knowing they were there gave me such strength.

'I think probably kindness is my number one attribute in a human being. I'll put it before any of the things like courage or bravery, or generosity or anything else….Kindness, that simple word. To be kind – it covers everything, to my mind. If you're kind, that's it.' (Roald Dahl).

I'll finish with this lovely poem by Shane:-

Vision

'Look for goodness
in the beautiful faces

See how love makes you
more beautiful

A lasting beauty
not like the fleeting of light
on the windblown hillside

But one that is etched in eternity

Remembered before and beyond time

See how they treat each other
with kindness and gentleness

Stay with the lovers arms
round the circles
of remembrance'

Regrets, I've had a few; too many to mention. Life is very short. Make the most of it and be kind.